A FIELD GUIDE TO PLANET EARTH

Projects for Reading Rocks, Rivers, Mountains, and the Forces That Shape Them

PAUL HILSTON

AND

CHRISTINE ROHN HILSTON

CHICAGO REVIEW PRESS

Library of Congress Cataloging-in-Publication Data
Hilston, Paul.
    A field guide to planet earth : projects for reading rocks, rivers,
mountains, and the forces that shape them / Paul Hilston and Christine
Rohn Hilston.
        p.   cm.
    "A Ziggurat book."
    Includes index.
    Summary: Provides practical information and hands-on activities
about earth science topics, including maps, water, soil, minerals, fossils,
and career possibilities.
        ISBN 1-55652-198-7
        1. Earth sciences—Juvenile literature.   [1. Earth science.]
I. Hilston, Christine Rohn.   II. Title.
QE29.H9   1993
550—dc20   93-8740
                                                                      CIP
                                                                       AC

For our children,
Erik, Brent, Beth, and Jacob

First Edition
Published by Chicago Review Press, Incorporated
814 North Franklin Street, Chicago, Illinois 60610

ISBN 1-55652-198-7
Printed in the United States of America

5 4 3 2 1

Contents

Chapter One

The Scoop on Earth Science

··

What do you think of when you hear "earth science?" Is it someone on an expedition in the mountains chipping rock samples from a cliff with a geology hammer? Someone searching for fossils in those rocks? Someone at a work table using satellite photographs and computers to compose maps? Or do you think of the weather forecaster on your local television station? Or a scientist performing chemical analyses of water samples aboard a research vessel that's rolling in a heavy sea? How about an agricultural agent helping a farmer determine what materials will improve the texture of his soil? Or an engineer calculating whether the ground and bedrock below will support a skyscraper? Maybe you think of someone flying an airplane into a hurricane to gather data on wind velocity? Or a scientist predicting where and when the next earthquake will occur? A gem cutter deciding how best to shape a gem for a particular piece of jewelry?

They're all good choices. Geologists, paleontologists, cartographers, meteorologists, oceanographers, pedologists, engineers, geographers, seismologists, gemologists—all these people are involved with some aspect of earth science. But earth science is also backyard rock collecting, checking the soil before planting a garden, and making a neighborhood map.

If you're thinking that earth science is a broad area, you're right. Although geology is probably the science that people most often associate with it, earth science involves all of the other sciences that deal with the earth or one of its parts. Earth science uses physics, chemistry, and biology to study our planet's lands, seas, atmosphere, climate, and position in space. It helps determine where people live and what they do there. It includes our environment and how we handle it.

Earth science ties together a lot of subjects—math, chemistry, physics, biology, geology, history, language, geography. In school, most subjects are taught separately: mathematics, science, social studies, English. And then they are divided one or more times into what seem like easy-to-describe categories. For example, science may be split into biology, chemistry, physics, and so on. But in real-life situations, the divisions among sciences or among subjects are not definite. To understand physics, for example, requires mathematical knowledge. It takes knowledge of certain chemical reactions to understand some biological processes. And to understand almost any subject requires knowledge of a language (in our case, English) to handle written material. Earth science is no exception; it builds on many other areas of knowledge.

Earth science investigations—whether performed by you or a scientist—are real-life, hands-on adventures. They may combine several sciences or types of activities. For instance, searching for meteorites or meteoritic dust includes some astronomy, some chemistry and physics, some geology and geography, and language. Ultimately, earth science investigators hope to learn more about our earth.

Among the things that make up earth science, geology and geography are especially important. *Geology* means "science of the earth." *Geography* means "description of the earth." You can't fully study geology unless you know the layout of the earth (geography). And you can't fully study geography unless you're familiar with the geological processes that shaped the land. If this sounds like talking in circles, it is. You can't isolate one area from another—everything is related.

How can you get involved in earth science? Think about this: No matter where you are, there's earth beneath your feet. It may be several stories below, or you may be standing directly on it. (Even if you're on a boat, the water beneath its hull is part of the earth. And somewhere below that water is land.) Whether you live in a city apartment or an isolated rural area, you're connected to earth science—when you check the weather forecast, for example, or choose a site to plant a garden.

You don't have to live in the shadow of a volcano, on the edge of a fault, near a coal mine, or on a mountainside to experience and explore earth science. You don't have to travel cross-country or around the world to learn the lay of the land. If you live in one of these places or are able to travel, that's great! But on the other hand, you can have fun with earth science in your own environment, your own backyard.

Do you like to get down and get your hands dirty? How about playing in the water and getting wet? Or would you rather stay clean? Do you want to be like Sherlock Holmes, looking for clues—evidence of past and present geologic activity? Do you dream of making a discovery that no one else has? How about answering a question that puzzles local citizens?

In this book we'll present some ideas for earth science exploration—some simple, some more complicated. You'll find background information as well as suggestions for projects and activities. Follow the activities as written, do some or all of them, substitute materials or tools if you need to, or use them as a springboard for designing your own. Remember to use common sense and take safety seriously (i.e., use protective eyewear when breaking rocks, wear gloves when handling sharp objects, etc.).

Because the scope of earth science is so broad, we're going to concentrate on its geological and geographical parts. In the following chapters, we'll take a look at *topography* (the shape and features of the earth's surface), erosion and weathering, mapmaking, soil, rocks and minerals, meteorites, and fossils. In the process, we'll use a simple stream table, make mud balls, draw maps, crack a few rocks, and examine fossils. We'll also introduce ideas about careers in the earth science field and show you where to get more information.

Some of these activities will point out how something that happens in one place—such as pollution—can affect another place, a larger area, or a future time. No matter where we are, we're all part of the same earth.

In spite of what somebody might have told you or what you may have thought, earth science is *not* boring. No matter how you choose to use this book, have fun!

Chapter Two

Maps
They Do More than Get You from Here to There

When was the last time you looked at a map? Today? Yesterday? It probably wasn't more than a couple of days ago. Was it the globe sitting on the corner of your desk? A map in a textbook? Did you consult a road map for directions? How about a map scrawled on a scrap of paper? Did you watch the weather broadcast on the television news?

We use maps nearly every day for a variety of purposes. And there are plenty of maps around in addition to the plain, folded-paper road map. Most of us have access to atlases, globes, and even computer software maps.

Maps and mapmakers appear to date back to the earliest ages of human history. The oldest known map of any kind is on a clay tablet. It depicts the Euphrates River flowing through northern Mesopotamia and has been dated at 3800 B.C. The oldest printed map in the world is one of western China dated 1115 A.D.

Early maps, whether drawn on rocks, on animal skins, or even in the dirt, defined territory and ownership. More than two thousand years before Christ, the Babylonians surveyed land holdings on clay tablets, known as cadastral maps. Rock-carving maps, like that of the Val Camonica in Italy, date from the second and first millennia B.C. The Val Camonica map shows stepped square fields, rivers, and dwellings.

People of all cultures and periods apparently needed and used maps. Imagine early people drawing crude maps in the dirt. They needed to know where the best hunting grounds were, the best routes around enemy territory, the way to the water hole. Artifacts like rock-carving maps and cadastral maps show that people of ancient times possessed the skill to draw maps. Even these people recognized that "a picture is worth a thousand words."

Of course, clay-tablet maps and rock maps are not as accurate as modern maps produced with the help of aerial photography, satellite imagery, electronic imaging, and computer digitization.

Modern mapmaking, or *cartography,* can be traced to thirteenth-century western Europe. Maps produced there were based upon measurement and were practical for use by travelers. The earliest surviving nautical charts and road maps date from the second half of the thirteenth century. Italian portolan charts—sets of sailing instructions on parchment—were created around 1250. In 1492, two men in Germany made the first modern terrestrial globe, 20 inches (50.8 centimeters) in diameter.

Improvements in the accuracy of measurement as well as in printing spurred advances in cartography. Topography and altitude could be accurately represented, and it was now possible for mapmakers to add color detail to their works.

Early in its history, the United States government became involved in cartography when George Washington appointed a geographer and surveyor to the Continental Army in 1777 to "take sketches of the country." Seven years later, Thomas Jefferson proposed the first official large-scale U.S. surveying and mapping program, which led to the creation of the General Land Office. The United States Geological Survey (USGS) conducted topographic surveying and mapping programs from the time it was formed in 1879.

During World War I, aerial photography was used for military intelligence. It soon became apparent that maps could be made from aerial photos, a development that continues to influence mapmaking to this day. Since World War II, cartographers have used increasingly sophisticated measuring techniques, satellites, and computer technology to produce all kinds of maps.

Today digitized map data are stored and manipulated by computers. Computer cartographers generate on-screen map displays that can be instantly modified by enlarging, reducing, and isolating sections of them. They can make data quickly available to other computer cartographers around the world. Computerized map data can be analyzed in an endless variety of ways. Compared with other mapmaking techniques, computerization considerably shortens the four to five years it once took to produce a map by hand from aerial or satellite images.

We are now a world awash in maps. In the last five hundred years we have mapped virtually every square foot of land, and much of the oceans and heavens as well. Besides road maps, there are geological maps, history maps, weather maps, military maps, census maps, agricultural maps, treasure maps, nautical charts, aeronautical charts—the list goes on and on.

Maps are so much a part of our everyday lives that people sometimes think they are more real than the real world. In 1962, astronaut John Glenn informed NASA's Mission Control, "I can see the whole state of Florida, laid out just like on a map." This statement also tells us that our maps are incredibly accurate.

The United States government has some thirty-nine federal agencies involved in making maps. Together, these agencies have produced nearly a quarter of a million different maps. The twelve largest mapmaking agencies distribute more than 161 million copies of their maps annually. That's just the U.S. federal government. Each year, Rand McNally, the world's largest nongovernment mapmaker, sells about 400 million maps, atlases, and globes. The American Automobile Association distributes about 35 million maps and 215 million individualized "Trip Tik" route maps each year. The total output of maps, globes, atlases, and related products appears to be over half a billion copies a year in the U.S. alone.

Libraries stock many maps. If the seventy largest collections of maps in private and public libraries were combined, there would be nearly 20 million maps and about 22 million aerial photographs.

Even with computers and satellite imagery to help make today's highly accurate maps, we still have one nagging problem that has plagued mapmakers for over five hundred years: How can you take something that is ball-shaped and make it flat without distortion?

In 1569, during the great period of world exploration, the Flemish geographer Gerardus Mercator introduced a flat map that was ideal for navigation on the high seas. On a Mercator map, or Mercator projection, any straight line is a line of constant true bearing. This map made it possible for a ship's captain or navigator to plot a straight-line course between any two points. The problem with Mercator's map, however, is that it distorts large shapes and greatly exaggerates the size of landmasses in the high latitudes. Mercator's map made Greenland larger than South America when it actually is only one-eighth the size of South America. His map showed North America (19 million square kilometers) almost the same size as Africa (30 million square kilometers). Mercator's projection also made Alaska and Brazil equal in size when Brazil is actually six times larger.

Two hundred and thirty-six years later in 1805, a German mathematician named Karl B. Mollweide came up with an equal-area map. His map depicted all regions on the earth in correct relative size. However, lands at higher latitudes are elongated or warped. Mollweide's map has proved most useful in comparing distribution of populations, religions, etc.

In 1904, Alphons van der Grinten came up with a map that had little distortion. In the high latitudes it avoided the extreme exaggeration of areas on the Mercator projection and the extreme compressing and shearing of Mollweide's map. One trouble, though, was that it showed Canada and the states of the former Soviet Union—already large areas—at more than twice their size.

A newer map, Arthur Robinson's projection, came out in 1963. In the combination of shape and area, it corresponds more closely to relative size than did van der Grinten's model. Robinson's map depicts Canada and the states of the former Soviet Union at about one and a half times their size. Most world maps today are of the Robinson shape.

To correct Mercator's perspective, which emphasized the Northern Hemisphere in general and Europe in particular (it's at the center of his map), German historian Arno Peters produced his world map in 1974. The Peters map shows all countries, continents, and oceans according to their actual size (although shapes are distorted). Accurate size comparisons are possible with Peters's map. It hasn't caught on with cartographers and geographers, but it did interest the United Nations. The U.N. helped fund development of a color world map based on Peters's projection.

In the following activity—mapping your bedroom, another room, or a small area—you won't need to worry about distortion at high latitudes, however.

• •

PROJECT

Map Your World

You are the cartographer for this project. Your task is to create an accurate map of your room or some other area of your home.

MATERIALS:

- Large square piece of cardboard, about 2 feet by 2 feet (18 inches by 18 inches is okay, too)
- Typing paper
- Straight pins
- Two coins or other flat objects
- Ruler
- Pencil
- Tape (masking tape, cellophane tape, etc.)

PROCEDURE:

1. Determine the scale for your map. Choose whether you will work with English or metric measure (that is, inches or centimeters). If the room you are mapping is large, the scale may be as large as 1 to 100. For a smaller room, it may be 1 to 20. On a 1 to 20 scale, this means that each inch (or centimeter, depending upon which you chose) on your map will equal 20 inches (or 20 centimeters) in the room.

   Note: The following instructions are given for a scale of 1 inch to 20 inches. If your scale is metric, adjust all references to inches to read centimeters. If the scale is larger, adjust all references to 20 to read 50, 100, or whatever you have chosen.

2. Tape your piece of paper to the middle of the piece of cardboard.

3. Make two pencil dots 1 inch apart in the center of the paper. This is the baseline on your map.

4. Place a straight pin in each dot just far enough into the cardboard so it is held there and doesn't fall out.

   Caution: To guard against sticking or scratching yourself with the sharp ends of the pins, do not push the pins all the way through the cardboard.

5. In the center of your room, place two flat objects (coins, for instance) 20 inches apart. They represent the marked dots on your paper. This is the baseline for your room.

6. Place one of the points on the paper over the corresponding point in your room. Keep the cardboard flat and do not move it.

7. Place the ruler on the paper next to the pin and sight along the edge of the ruler to one of the corners of the room.

8. Draw a faint line along the edge of the ruler to the end of the paper.

9. Repeat steps 7 and 8 for each corner of the room and for major objects in the room.

   IMPORTANT: Do not move the cardboard or paper or other large objects in your room.

10. After you have drawn lines from one point to all corners of the room, move the cardboard with paper and pins attached so the other marked point is over its corresponding point in the room.

11. Repeat steps 7, 8, and 9 for this second marked point.

12. Where the lines that you have drawn intersect are the corners of your room and the locations of other major objects. Mark these

crossing points well, remove the straight pins, and erase the rest of the faint lines you drew.

13. Connect the outer dots on the paper to draw the outline of the room.

● ●

You can use this procedure to map outdoor areas, too—your yard, a portion of your yard, a playground. Treasure map, anyone?

Chapter Three

Topographic Maps
···

Remember how often the coyote in cartoons runs wildly along the countryside pursuing the elusive roadrunner—only to arrive at a cliff the coyote hadn't planned on encountering? And we all know what happens next!

Have you ever driven down a road wondering what was just over the hill off to one side or the other? Have you ever started out on a trail that looked level, but then made some twists and turns, and pretty soon you were climbing a steep slope that you didn't realize was there? Have you ever wanted to fish in a river or stream at a location other than its intersection with a major highway?

We look at photographs of an area, but we only see what was facing the camera and within its angle of view. We see a railroad track disappear behind a hill in the distance. We stand at the top of a cliff and wonder how large a drop it is to the valley below. We stand at the base of a hill and wonder what we could see from its top. And if it's private property or otherwise off-limits, we can't travel to it to take a look.

Often we don't know what lies on the other side of the mountain or on the land isolated by the creek. It may be impractical or impossible to explore the area alone. But we can learn what is there; we can get an idea of the location's terrain and relief by examining a *topographic map* of the area. If only the coyote had consulted a topographic map first!

Topographic maps are the workhorses of cartography. They are planning tools. They are used by people planning airports, highways, dams, pipelines, and almost any type of building. They are essential in ecological studies, environmental control, geological research, seismology, water-quality studies, flood control, conservation, and other fields. In other words, people in a wide variety of engineering and scientific professions use topographic maps.

People participating in leisure activities also consult topographic maps. They are valuable route-planning and location-scouting tools for hikers, bikers, hunters, runners, fishers, and campers.

Topographic maps are also important because they form the basis for other types of maps, including road maps, park and forest maps, geological maps, and even aviation charts.

Topographic maps use lines, colors, and symbols to represent natural and man-made features. On a topographic map, brown or reddish brown contour lines connect points of equal elevation to show the precise shape and elevation of the land. Contour lines that are tightly packed together, for instance, indicate steep terrain since the elevation changes rapidly in a short distance. Topographic maps show the location and shape of mountains, lakes, rivers, creeks, and trails, as well as man-made objects such as railroads, highways, dirt roads, cemeteries, mines, trails, and buildings. Symbols and colors are important parts of topographic maps.

Types of Topographic Maps

Topographic maps are classified according to scale, which is expressed numerically—for instance, 1:24,000. This is read as "one to twenty-four thousand." This means that 1 unit (inch, centimeter, foot, etc.) on the map equals 24,000 of that same unit on the ground.

Large-scale maps (1:24,000) are useful when detailed information is needed, such as for engineering planning. Recreational users—hikers, campers, etc.—also use large-scale topographic maps often. Intermediate-scale maps (1:50,000 to 1:100,000) cover larger areas and are used for land management and planning. Small-scale maps (1:250,000 to 1:1,000,000) are used for overviews of extensive projects and regional planning because they cover very large areas.

The United States Geological Survey (USGS) periodically updates its approximately sixty thousand topographic maps that cover the entire country. Each topographic map, regardless of scale, covers a specific *quadrangle*—a four-sided area bounded by parallels of latitude and meridians of longitude. Each of the USGS's five series of topographic maps covers a different-sized quadrangle and is on a different scale.

1. 7.5-minute series

   • Large-scale maps
   • Each quadrangle is 7.5 minutes square (1 minute equals $\frac{1}{60}$ degree of

latitude or longitude)
- Scale is 1:24,000 (Alaska is 1:25,000; Puerto Rico is 1:20,000)
- 1 inch represents about 2,000 feet

2. 15-minute series
   - Intermediate-scale maps
   - Each quadrangle is 15 minutes square
   - Scale is 1:62,500 (Alaska is 1:63,360)
   - 1 inch equals about 1 mile

3. Intermediate-scale series
   - Each quadrangle is 30 minutes (0.5 degree) by 1 degree
   - Scale is 1:100,000
   - 1 inch equals about 1.5 miles

4. U.S. 1:250,000 series
   - Small-scale maps
   - Each quadrangle is 1 degree by 2 degrees
   - 1 inch equals 4 miles (Alaska and Hawaii are on different scales)

5. International Map of the World series
   - Small-scale maps
   - Each quadrangle is 4 degrees by 6 degrees
   - Scale is 1:1,000,000
   - 1 inch equals 16 miles

Large-scale maps are best for our purposes, so we'll use the 7.5-minute series. Each map is 7.5 minutes on each side with a 1:24,000 scale. But, you say, the map isn't square. We may refer to the area as 7.5 minutes square, but the topographic maps are not geometrically square. What gives? Remember that a degree of longitude is not the same distance as a degree of latitude, and the width of a degree of longitude changes as you move from the equator toward the poles. Nor is the earth perfectly spherical. These factors have plagued mapmakers since cartography began.

Symbols and Colors

Check out the list of topographic symbols for the different things you can locate on a topographic map. Here are just some of them: shape of landforms, elevation above sea level, bodies of water, roads, railroads, buildings (you can find your home if you're in a rural or semirural area), power transmission lines, political boundaries, wooded areas, swamps, parks of all sizes, cemeteries, airports, etc.

TOPOGRAPHIC MAP SYMBOLS

VARIATIONS WILL BE FOUND ON OLDER MAPS

Primary highway, hard surface . . . .

Secondary highway, hard surface . . . .

Light-duty road, hard or improved surface . . . .

Unimproved road . . . .

Road under construction, alinement known . . . .

Proposed road . . . .

Dual highway, dividing strip 25 feet or less . . . .

Dual highway, dividing strip exceeding 25 feet . . . .

Trail . . . .

Railroad: single track and multiple track . . . .

Railroads in juxtaposition . . . .

Narrow gage: single track and multiple track . . . .

Railroad in street and carline . . . .

Bridge: road and railroad . . . .

Drawbridge: road and railroad . . . .

Footbridge . . . .

Tunnel: road and railroad . . . .

Overpass and underpass . . . .

Small masonry or concrete dam . . . .

Dam with lock . . . .

Dam with road . . . .

Canal with lock . . . .

Buildings (dwelling, place of employment, etc.) . . . .

School, church, and cemetery . . . . Cem

Buildings (barn, warehouse, etc.) . . . .

Power transmission line with located metal tower . . . .

Telephone line, pipeline, etc. (labeled as to type) . . . .

Wells other than water (labeled as to type) . . . . Oil . . . . Gas

Tanks: oil, water, etc. (labeled only if water) . . . . Water

Located or landmark object; windmill . . . .

Open pit, mine, or quarry; prospect x

Shaft and tunnel entrance . . . .

Horizontal and vertical control station:

Tablet, spirit level elevation . . . . BM △ 5653

Other recoverable mark, spirit level elevation . . . . △ 5455

Horizontal control station: tablet, vertical angle elevation VABM △ 95/9

Any recoverable mark, vertical angle or checked elevation △ 3775

Vertical control station: tablet, spirit level elevation . . . . . BM × 957

Other recoverable mark, spirit level elevation . . . . × 954

Spot elevation . . . . × 7369   × 7369

Water elevation 670   670

Boundaries: National . . . .

State . . . .

County, parish, municipio . . . .

Civil township, precinct, town, barrio . . . .

Incorporated city, village, town, hamlet . . . .

Reservation, National or State . . . .

Small park, cemetery, airport, etc. . . . .

Land grant . . . .

Township or range line, United States land survey . . . . . .

Township or range line, approximate location . . . .

Section line, United States land survey . . . .

Section line, approximate location . . . .

Township line, not United States land survey . . . .

Section line, not United States land survey . . . .

Found corner: section and closing . . . .

Boundary monument: land grant and other . . . .

Fence or field line . . . .

Index contour . . . .   Intermediate contour . .

Supplementary contour   Depression contours . .

Fill . . . .   Cut . . . .

Levee . . . .   Levee with road . . . . .

Mine dump . . . .   Wash . . . .

Tailings . . . .   Tailings pond . . . .

Shifting sand or dunes   Intricate surface . . . .

Sand area . . . .   Gravel beach . . . .

Perennial streams . . . .   Intermittent streams . .

Elevated aqueduct . . . .   Aqueduct tunnel . . . . .

Water well and spring . . . . .   Glacier . . . .

Small rapids . . . .   Small falls . . . .

Large rapids . . . .   Large falls . . . .

Intermittent lake . . . .   Dry lake bed . . . .

Foreshore flat . . . .   Rock or coral reef . . . .

Sounding, depth curve . . . .   Piling or dolphin . . . . .

Exposed wreck . . . .   Sunken wreck . . . .

Rock, bare or awash; dangerous to navigation . . . .

Marsh (swamp) . . . .   Submerged marsh . . . .

Wooded marsh . . . .   Mangrove . . . .

Woods or brushwood . .   Orchard . . . .

Vineyard . . . .   Scrub . . . .

Land subject to controlled inundation . . . .   Urban area . . . .

Figure 3-1. Topographic map symbols. *(Courtesy of U.S. Geological Survey)*

Colors are important, too. They make it quick and easy to pick out wooded areas, bodies of water, or urban areas. The following colors appear on topographic maps.

- *Blue*—Bodies of water like lakes, rivers, streams, ponds, swamps, drainage ditches
- *Black*—Man-made objects like small roads, railroads, buildings (factories, homes, schools, churches, stores), transmission lines, political boundaries
- *Green*—Wooded areas, orchards
- *Red*—Important roads
- *Pink*—Heavily built-up areas larger than ¾ square mile
- *Purple*—New features added as a result of aerial photography when map was last updated
- *Brown*—Contour lines that indicate shape and elevation of the land's surface

The symbol chart (Figure 3-1) and the Lorain (Ohio) Quadrangle map (Figures 3-2 and 3-3 are reprinted here in black and white, so the colors show as shades of gray. If you obtain your own copies from the USGS or Canada Map Office, you'll be able to see the colors.

Topographic map reading is fun and interesting. Get a map of your immediate location or of somewhere you'd like to learn more about. United States topographic maps and symbol lists are available from the USGS distribution centers (addresses are in the Appendix) or from local suppliers. You can obtain Canadian topographic maps from the Canada Map Office (address also in the Appendix). Or check with outdoor equipment stores and wilderness outfitters. They often carry a selection of topographic maps because of their value to outdoor enthusiasts.

• •

PROJECT

Interpreting a Topographic Map

Look at the Lorain (Ohio) Quadrangle reprinted in Figure 3-2 (northern section) and Figure 3-3 (southern section) at a reduced size. It's a 7.5-minute series map with a 1:24,000 scale. When you've studied this map and found the following information, you can get your own full-size map and answer similar questions about it.

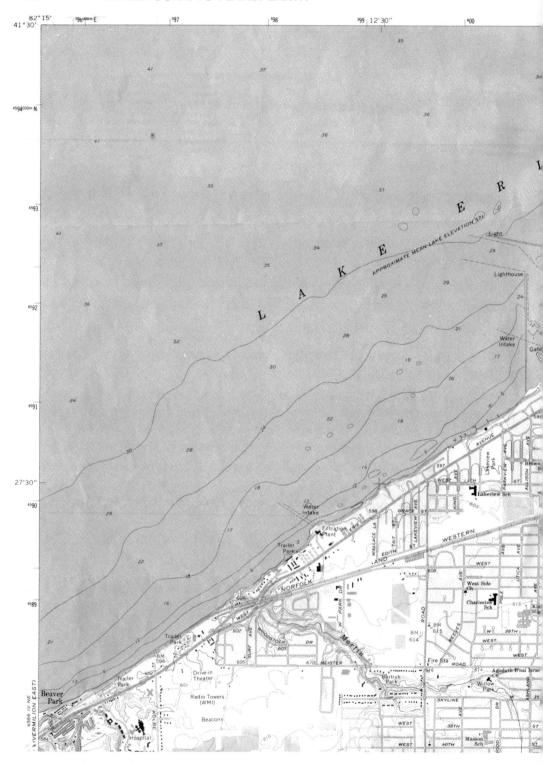

Figure 3-2. Northern portion of 7.5-minute series Lorain (Ohio) Quadrangle. *(Courtesy of U.S. Geological Survey)*

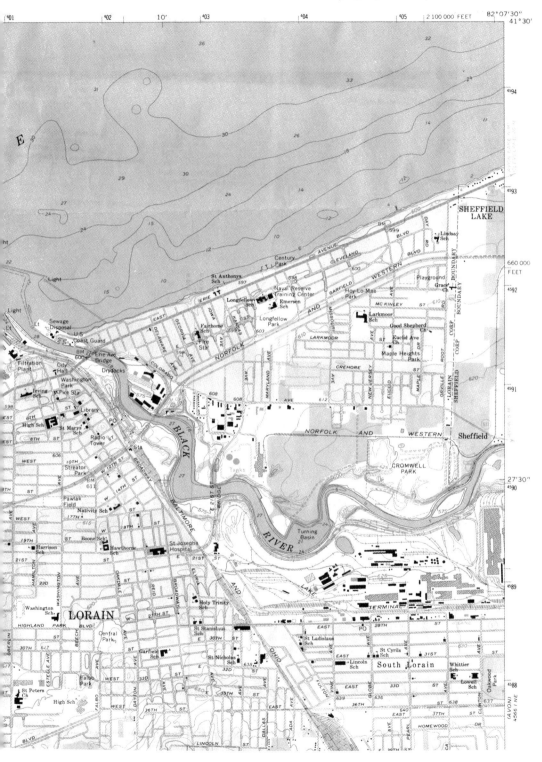

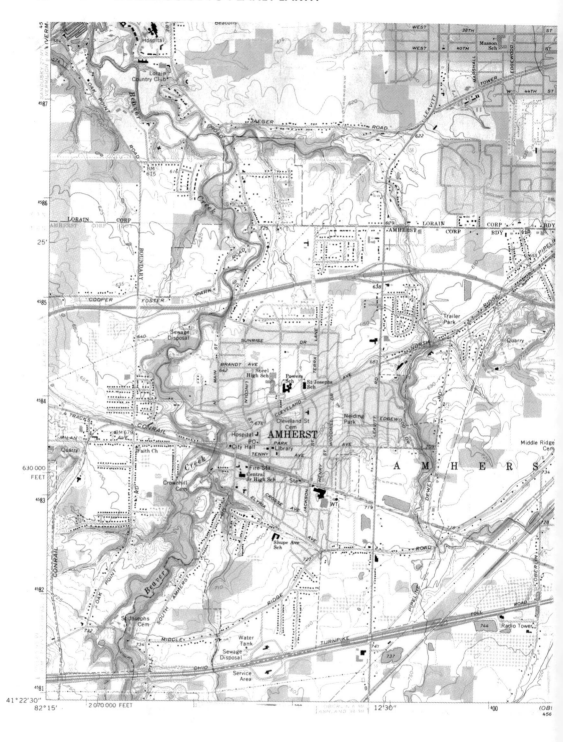

Figure 3-3. Southern portion of Lorain (Ohio) Quadrangle. *(Courtesy of U.S. Geological Survey)*

MATERIALS:

- Topographic map
- Scratch paper
- Pencil
- Ruler
- String

PROCEDURE:

Find the following information on the Lorain Quadrangle, then determine similar information from a topographic map of your own choosing.

1. Determine latitude and longitude of the map. When you know latitude and longitude, you can precisely locate the area on the globe or on a continental or world map.
   a. Numbers are printed at the four corners of the map. On the map as reprinted here, look at the upper corners of the northern section and the lower corners of the southern section. Begin at the upper left corner, which says 41°30'00" and 82°15'00".The first number is latitude; the second is longitude. This is read as "forty-one degrees, thirty minutes, and zero seconds latitude, by eighty-two degrees, fifteen minutes, and zero seconds longitude." Look at the other three corners and find the latitude and longitude of the map.
   b. The southern latitude of the map is 41°22'30".
   c. What is the northern latitude of the map?
   d. What is the eastern longitude of the map?
   e. What is the western longitude of the map?
   f. How many degrees, minutes, and seconds are there between the latitudes of the map's northern and southern limits? Between the longitudes of the map's eastern and western boundaries? (Remember, this is a 7.5-minute series map.)
2. If you want details of areas adjacent to the Lorain Quadrangle, what maps (quadrangles) would you need to obtain?
   a. Look at the right margin of the Lorain Quadrangle's northern section. Find the word *Avon*. That is the quadrangle that adjoins the Lorain Quadrangle to the center right, or east.
   b. The name of the map that adjoins the Lorain Quadrangle (southern section) to the lower right is Grafton. It is in the compass direction of southeast.
   c. What is the name of the map that adjoins the Lorain Quadrangle to the lower center? What compass direction is that?

d. What is the name of the map that adjoins the Lorain Quadrangle to the lower left? What compass direction is that?

e. What is the name of the map that adjoins the Lorain Quadrangle to the left center? What compass direction is that?

f. What map adjoins the Lorain Quadrangle to the upper right, upper center, and upper left? Why?

3. To identify smaller areas on a topographic map, divide it into nine rectangles. See the drawing in Figure 3-4 to name them. Using the Lorain Quadrangle as reprinted here, R1, R2, R3, and the top halves of R4, R5, and R6 will be in the northern section. The bottom halves of R4, R5, R6, and all of R7, R8, and R9 will be in the southern section.

R1	R2	R3
R4	R5	R6
R7	R8	R9

Figure 3-4. Nine rectangles of a topographic map.

Using this system with the Lorain Quadrangle, locate the following places by rectangle designations.

a. West Recreation Field

b. Amherst

c. Beaver Park

d. Clearview School

e. U.S. Coast Guard

f. Naval Reserve Training Center

g. Middle Ridge Cemetery

4. Locate the representative fraction or scale of the topographic map. (It's below rectangle R8.) Locate the graphic scale. (It also appears below the map.)

a. What is the scale?

b. Measure the graphic scale with a ruler.
   - 1 inch = __?__ miles on the map.
   - 1 inch = __?__ feet on the map.
   - 1 inch = __?__ kilometers.

c. What is the distance (in miles or kilometers) between Clearview School and Crestwood School?

d. Measure the distance between BM 766 in R9 and the Lorain

Country Club in R4. You may want to use a piece of string. What is the actual distance?

5. With the help of the topographic map symbol list (Figure 3-1), find the following things on the Lorain Quadrangle:

- A railroad
- A building
- A lighthouse
- A school
- A church
- An orchard
- A water tank

See how many other symbols you can locate and identify on the topographic map.

6. Contour lines join points of equal height above sea level. They're the curved and looped lines shown in brown or reddish brown on topographic maps. In Figures 3-2 and 3-3, they appear as thin black lines. We can learn several things from contour lines, such as how high above sea level the land is and the shape of the land—hills, valleys, cliffs, flat land, etc. The *contour interval* is the difference in height between two consecutive contour lines. In non-mountainous areas the contour interval can be 5 or 10 feet, in hilly areas 10 to 100 feet, and in mountainous areas it can be 100 feet or greater. At the bottom center (R8) of the map, you will find the contour interval.

a. What is the contour interval on the Lorain Quadrangle?

In R5 (southern section), just above the words *Elmwood Cemetery* you will find a contour line numbered 650. That means that all points on the contour line are 650 feet above sea level. Notice that the thicker contour lines have their elevations printed on them. To determine the elevation of a narrow contour line, start with a labeled contour line and add 5 feet for each line if going uphill or subtract 5 feet for each line if going downhill. On other topographic maps, add or subtract the appropriate contour interval.

b. To find out which way is uphill and which way is downhill, find a few of the thicker lines with marked elevations and compare them. In which general direction on the Lorain Quadrangle does elevation increase? As you move from Lake Erie at the top of the map (north) toward the bottom of the map (south) the elevation rises.

c. When contour lines form a circular shape with rings inside each other, they show a hill. Locate a hill in R7 on the Lorain Quadrangle. (It's just to the lower right of the word *Amherst*. The word *Ave.* is almost on top of the hill.)

d. The closer contour lines are together, the steeper the slope of the land is. Look along Beaver Creek in R7 or the Black River in R3 to locate valleys with steep sloping sides.

e. To indicate a hole rather than a hill, contour lines will be drawn with short perpendicular lines (hachure marks), like ⊥⊥⊥⊥⊥⊥⊥⊥⊥⊥⊥⊥⊥⊥. Locate this feature on the Lorain Quadrangle at the bottom of R6 or top of R9 between Lake Ave. and the Radio Tower.

f. The letters BM followed by a number and ● or X indicate a *bench mark*. Bench marks are points at which the elevation is checked periodically by the USGS. The number is the exact elevation of the bench mark. Find a bench mark in R6 on the southern portion of the Lorain Quadrangle. (It's near the side of the map just north of the word *Sheffield* printed vertically.) What is the elevation?

g. Determine the lowest elevation on the Lorain Quadrangle. (Remember that this particular topographic map has a contour interval of 5 feet.)

h. What is the highest point on this map?

i. Determine the elevations of the following:
   • Crestwood School
   • Central Park in the city of Lorain
   • Filtration plant along Lake Erie
   • Approximate mean Lake Erie elevation

j. In Lake Erie, the contour lines are shown in blue on a topographical map (because they're in water), and the contour interval is not 5 feet. It is 6 feet.
   • What is the deepest part of Lake Erie shown on the Lorain Quadrangle?
   • What is the deepest point of the Black River on this map?

● ●

Ordering Topographic Maps

The USGS publishes a series of indexes to topographic maps (as well as geological and general maps) that are helpful in locating the map you are looking for. There is a separate index of topographic maps for each state and an index for the national park system. The USGS also publishes indexes by map scale (small, medium, and large scale) for maps covering the entire United States. The USGS indexes, price lists, and order forms are available free upon request; maps themselves must be purchased. (Canadian topographic maps are available from the Canada Map Office.)

These materials are available from the distribution centers listed in the "Finding Maps" section of this book's Appendix, as well as from commercial map dealers.

Chapter Four

What a Relief!

Relief Maps

When you unfold or unroll a paper map, it is flat. Run your finger over it. You don't feel any roughness or bumps; you feel the paper's smooth surface. By clever use of color and shading, however, flat maps can give the world a three-dimensional look. Maps indicating a three-dimensional view using relative elevations are *relief* maps.

Flat maps that are colored and shaded to represent our three-dimensional world are called *visual relief* maps. They often show lower elevations in shades of green and higher elevations in a variety of browns. There may be a large visual relief map in your classroom. If not, look at an atlas. Some globes also indicate relief with color and shading.

Topographic maps are a special variety of relief map. Each topographic map covers a *quadrangle,* a four-sided area bounded by parallels of latitude and meridians of longitude. A topographic map doesn't look three-dimensional. Instead, it shows elevations quite precisely by means of *contour lines* that connect points of equal elevation. In addition, it shows trails, buildings, and other structures. Topographic maps are discussed in more detail in Chapter 3.

Raised relief maps actually are three-dimensional. Run your fingers across a raised relief map. You can actually feel the mountains, valleys, and plains. Raised relief maps are generally made of plastic, vinyl, or rubber. Plastic can be vacuum-formed with greater detail than rubber or vinyl maps, but rubber and vinyl are more durable.

■■■■■■■■■■■■■■■■■■■■■■■■■■■■■■■■■■■■

The largest map in the world is a relief map called the "Giant Relief Map of California." It's 450 feet by 18 feet (137 meters by 5.5 meters) and weighs 43 tons. From 1924 to 1962, the map was on display in the Ferry Building in San Francisco. It is now in storage.

■■■■■■■■■■■■■■■■■■■■■■■■■■■■■■■■■■■■

In the following project, you will construct a corrugated cardboard relief map. You'll need a topographic map as the basis for your relief map. You can use a topographic map of your location. Or, if you would like to make a relief map of a volcanic mountain, the Shasta (California) Quadrangle is a good map to use. If you'd like a flatter map with a river, you may want to use the Lorain (Ohio) Quadrangle. You can use the entire map or only a portion of it.

• •

PROJECT

How Do You Make Relief?

To make a raised relief map, you will need a lot of corrugated cardboard. If you don't have a stack of cardboard boxes at home, ask local stores—supermarkets, drug stores, and discount stores—for boxes they may be discarding.

MATERIALS:

- Corrugated cardboard
- Topographic map
- Tracing paper
- Pencil
- Good, sharp scissors (be careful!)
- All-purpose glue
- Masking tape

PROCEDURE:

1. Start with one piece of cardboard as the base of your relief map. Make it the same size as your topographic map or the area of the topographic map you want to use.
2. Find the contour line of lowest elevation on the topographic map. (Contour lines are printed in reddish brown on the topographic maps. They connect points of equal elevation.)
3. Tape tracing paper to the topographic map, making sure it covers the entire contour line of lowest elevation. This should be a large area on the map, so you may need to use more than one piece of tracing paper.
4. Trace the contour line of lowest elevation.

Figure 4-1. Tracing a contour line on a topographic map.

5. Remove the tracing paper from the topographic map and cut along the line you traced.

Figure 4-2. Cutting along traced line.

6. Place the cut-out tracing paper shape on a piece of cardboard. You may want to secure it with tape.

7. Trace the paper outline onto the cardboard.

8. Remove the tracing paper from the cardboard.

9. Cut the cardboard along the line you drew.

10. Place the cardboard cutout representing the area inside the contour line on top of your cardboard base in a position corresponding to the lowest contour line's position on the topographic map. Glue it in place.

11. Tape tracing paper to the topographic map, covering the next highest contour line.

12. Trace the contour line.

13. Remove the tracing paper and cut along the traced line.

14. Secure the tracing paper cutout on a piece of cardboard and draw the cutout's outline onto the cardboard.

15. Remove the tracing paper and cut the cardboard along the line you drew.

16. Place the cardboard cutout representing the area inside the contour line on top of the previous cardboard contour area on the cardboard base. Make sure it's in the correct position and glue it in place.

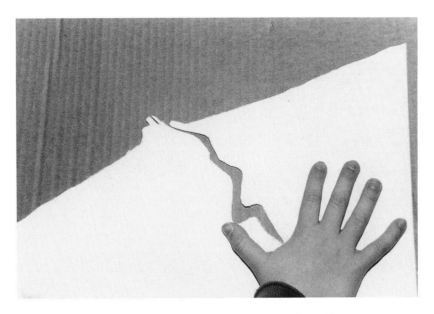

Figure 4-3. Gluing cardboard contour cutout onto cardboard base.

17. Repeat steps 11 through 16 for each contour line on the topographic map, working from lines of lower elevation to higher elevation. The last pieces of cardboard will be the smallest.

    Note: If your topographic map shows valleys, you will end up with more than one piece of cardboard for each contour line on the map.

● ●

Notice how natural features come to life on your relief map. You may decide to paint it or add other items, such as buildings, that are shown on the topographic map.

Chapter Five

How Does the Water Flow?
....

Drainage Basins

I f you drop a stick or homemade boat into a nearby river, stream, or
drainage ditch, which way does it go? Why? Where does it finally end
up (assuming it doesn't get snagged or grounded)? How many other
streams or rivers flow to the same body of water? What about rainwater
running in the street along the curb? Is flooding a serious problem in the
area?

The land area where all the water that drains into a stream comes from
makes up that stream's *drainage basin*. Likewise, the drainage basins of all
the streams that flow into a larger river make up the river's drainage basin.
The drainage basins of the rivers that drain into a lake make up the lake's
drainage basin. Even water in a parking lot, driveway, or street after a heavy
rain is part of a drainage basin. It flows in a consistent direction and
eventually reaches a stream or other body of water.

Planning a canoe trip? It's much easier to paddle downstream than up.
The following project can help you determine starting and ending points
for your journey. The land along a river's bank is relatively flat, but would it
be a good location to build a house? It looks fertile, too, but should you
plant a garden there? This project, together with those in Chapter 6, will
help determine a stream bank or riverbank's flooding potential. You'll also
calculate a drainage basin's approximate area—that is, how much land
surface drains water into a river, stream, or lake. For example, the drainage

basin of Lake Erie (the eleventh largest lake in the world as measured by surface area) covers 9,906 square miles (25,657 square kilometers).

You may want to think about calculating the volume of water flowing on an hourly, daily, or annual basis. Be sure to check out the other follow-up suggestions.

● ●

PROJECT

Drawing a Drainage Basin

This project will help you draw the shape of a local drainage basin and calculate its approximate area.

MATERIALS:

- Local topographic map (You can use a local highway map if it shows streams and rivers.)
- Ruler
- Two different-colored pencils
- Large sheet of tracing paper
- Removable tape, such as masking tape

Your state geological survey or county engineer's office (look for government listings in your phone directory) can tell you where to get a topographic map of your area. Many outfitters or stores that offer hiking and canoeing supplies sell topographic maps, too. You can order topographic maps by mail from the distribution centers listed in the "Finding Maps" section of the Appendix. Indexes of maps by state and price lists are free.

PROCEDURE:

1. If you are close to a stream or river that flows into a lake or larger river, locate it on your topographic map. If not, choose a creek, stream, or river on the map that flows into a larger creek, stream, river, or lake.
2. Tape the topographic map down onto a flat surface.
3. Cover the river, stream, or creek you've chosen with a piece of tracing paper. Call this your main river, stream, or creek.
4. Using a pencil (blue, maybe), trace the main river, stream, or creek from its *mouth* (the point where it flows into a lake or another river) back upstream to its *source* (beginning, headwater).

5. Now trace all the *tributaries* (branches that flow into the larger river or stream) of your main river, stream, or creek, including drainage ditches. Use arrows to show the direction of water flow.

6. After coloring all the water of your river, stream, or creek and its tributaries in one color, use another color to draw a line completely around the outside of all the tributaries and main river, stream, or creek.

7. To calculate the approximate surface area of the drainage basin, multiply its length times its width (each measured in kilometers or miles according to the map scale) to get the number of square kilometers or square miles in the drainage basin.

PROJECT

Mapping a Drainage Route

In this project you'll make a map of the water drainage route from your home to a stream, river, or lake.

MATERIALS:

- Large sheet of paper or detailed street map
- Colored pencils or markers
- Ruler
- City or topographic map for reference

PROCEDURE:

1. Mark your home near the center of the paper, or locate your home on a street map.

2. Using a colored pencil, draw the route that water flowing from your driveway or the street curb takes. Try to follow it until it reaches a river or lake.

   Note: At some point, city curbs will direct water into a storm sewer. You may want to contact your local sewer district to determine the water's route to the wastewater treatment plant. From there, you can follow its path into a stream, river, or larger body of water. In rural areas, storm water may enter drainage ditches that empty directly into a stream or river.

3. Using a different colored pencil or marker, trace the drainage route from a friend's or relative's home in another part of town. Notice

where the route intersects or joins the route of the water from your home.

● ●

As the water flows, so flows what's in it. Not only does that mean sticks or leaves (too many can dam up or alter the water's flow), it also means pollution. Agricultural chemicals, lawn and garden fertilizers and pesticides, oil leaking from automobiles, spilled fuel, other toxic substances—all can run off, entering the drainage system.

Weed killer from *one* lawn or a cup of spilled fuel doesn't sound like much. But when pollution from all sources in an area is added together, it can result in measurable or even harmful amounts in the drainage basin's water supply.

Some polluting substances may enter wastewater treatment plants, where removal is complicated or expensive. In other cases, substances enter rivers or lakes directly and disperse over a wide area. The cost of containment and cleanup is high, and environmental damage or health threats may result.

Notice how substances entering the drainage basin via a number of tributaries may snowball and potentially affect more people on the journey downstream.

Follow-Up Ideas:

• Launch a homemade wooden boat or marked piece of wood into one of the streams or creeks on your map—ideally in a public area. See how far you can follow the boat's journey downstream. Make sure you don't trespass on someone else's property. Note how long it takes to get from one point to another. Where does the water flow swiftly? Slowly?

• If any of the waterways on your topographic map are open for canoeing, plan and take a canoe trip through your drainage basin. Think safety and wear a life preserver.

• Think about how construction of a dam in a certain place would affect the drainage basin, both above and below the dam.

• Calculate the approximate water flow of a stream at a certain point. *Hint*: Water flow is usually measured in cubic feet per second (cfs).

• If you live in a city with storm sewers, contact the engineering office of your city or regional sewer district for a below-street flow diagram of sewer lines.

• Read *Paddle to the Sea,* by Holling Clancy Holling.

Chapter Six

Running Water
●●

Rivers, Waterfalls, and Dams

Running water fascinates people of all ages. Some like to sit quietly and listen to the babble of a small brook. The endless crashing of waves onto shore appeals to others. Some, wishing to experience the power and thrill of rushing water, join whitewater rafting or canoeing expeditions. Still others plan whole vacations around trips to rivers and waterfalls.

Each year, about 5 million visitors from all over the world come to see Niagara Falls. Niagara Falls isn't the largest waterfall in the world, but it's easily accessible and still quite impressive. Horseshoe Falls, the Canadian portion, is 173 feet high, 2,000 feet wide, and flows at a rate of 212,000 cubic feet per second (cfs). That's a lot of water passing before your eyes!

■■■

WATERFALLS AROUND THE WORLD

- The highest waterfall in the world is Angel Falls on the Rio Caroní in Venezuela. Discovered in 1935, it spills 3,212 feet (979 meters) down a sandstone cliff.

- Sete Quedas, or Guairá Falls, on the Paraná River in South America has the greatest water flow rate of any waterfall in the world. It checks in at 470,000 cfs.

- Boyoma Falls (Stanley Falls) in Africa consists of seven cataracts, each less than

10 feet (3 meters) high, spread over nearly 60 miles (96.5 kilometers) of the Congo River.
- Victoria Falls, on the Zambezi River between the countries of Zambia and Zimbabwe, is over 5,000 feet (1,524 meters) wide.
- Sutherland Falls, the highest waterfall in New Zealand, cascades 1,900 feet (579 meters) from Lake Quill into the Arthur River.

■■■■■■■■■■■■■■■■■■■■■■■■■■■■■■■■■■■■■■■

Scientists estimate that our planet contains 360 million cubic miles of water. At any given time, slightly more than 97 percent of the earth's water is in the oceans. A little more than 2 percent is frozen in icecaps and glaciers. The remainder—less than 1 percent—is in lakes, in rivers, underground, and in the atmosphere. Lakes hold .017 percent of the world's water; rivers hold only .0001 percent.

Yet all the rivers in the world, including even the laziest streams, constantly shape the earth's surface. They excavate valleys through erosion, transport soil and rocky debris, deposit new landforms, and rework their own channels. Gravity is behind rivers' work. It continuously pulls water downhill toward sea level, the ultimate destination of the world's water.

Compared to volcanoes and earthquakes, rivers shape the land slowly and peacefully. Yet, added together, rivers are a force more pervasive and powerful than the more violent agents of change. The changes a river makes in the land depend upon the speed of its flow, the slope and shape of its channel, and the type of material in its bed.

The fastest river velocities, of course, occur near waterfalls. As the Niagara River spills over Niagara Falls, for instance, it reaches a speed of 100 feet per second, or 68 miles (109 kilometers) per hour. Below Guairá Falls in South America, the Paraná River flows at 45 feet per second, or 30 miles (48 kilometers) per hour. On the average, however, streams flow at a rate of from 3 to 6 feet per second, or 2 to 4 miles (3 to 6 kilometers) per hour.

So it makes sense that rivers flow fastest in the steep mountains, right? Not always. In fact, the speed of a river often increases downstream despite the absence of the steep slopes that mountains provide. The reason for this anomaly is friction. In the mountains, a river is neither as deep nor as wide as it is downstream, so there is more riverbank area per volume of water. That means proportionally more of the water in the river must rub against its banks. Also, in the mountains comparatively less erosion has occurred, so the riverbanks tend to be rougher and less smoothed than they are downstream. All this creates more friction, which opposes the free movement of water. So the river runs slower than it would if friction were absent and only gravity were acting on the water flow.

As a river moves downstream, it joins with other streams and captures more runoff from its larger immediate drainage area. Although the slope of its path is less steep, the river is usually wider and deeper. Now a greater proportion of the water volume flows free of the friction caused by the sides and bottom of the riverbed.

Surprisingly, hydrologists (water scientists) have calculated that the water in a river can lose up to 97 percent of its energy to friction. This includes friction from the air above the water's surface, friction from the stream bed, and the turbulence of the water itself.

It has been estimated that even with this energy loss due to friction, flowing water can lower the level of land over the entire earth by as much as 3 inches (7.6 centimeters) per one thousand years. This suggests that the land will eventually be eroded away. However, other forces like uplifting and volcanoes are at work building up the earth's surface.

Rivers don't travel in straight lines. Rather, they tend to meander, or curve. They erode here, deposit there. Because they work slowly and constantly, the results of a river's action may not be apparent for years.

●●●●●●●●●●●●●●●●●●●●●●●●●●●●●●●●●●●●●

PROJECT

River Models: Stream Tables

When you were a child you observed the action of water upon sand in a sandbox. As you poured water the sand moved out of the way to form "ponds" and "rivers."

Because of difficulties and obstacles in observing rivers' effects in nature, hydrologists create river scenarios on a smaller scale in a laboratory or experimental setting. They use stream tables. By varying factors like slope, width, depth, and flow rate, hydrologists can predict what a real river is likely to do. They can study a river's shape, a waterfall, or shoreline erosion.

You can, too, by building your own stream table.

Base the size of your stream table upon the space you have and any materials you may already have on hand. Remember, it will be heavy when loaded with sand and water. You can place it atop a sturdy table or on several supports, like sawhorses, indoors or outdoors. Though it should be rectangular, it may be as small as 1 foot by 3 feet, 2 feet by 8 feet, or larger. The longer it is, the greater variety of stream action you can observe.

Caution: This activity requires the use of a saw and drill. Ask an adult for assistance. Wear safety goggles.

Note: Be sure to use your stream table in a place where spilled water or sand won't cause a problem.

MATERIALS:

- Plywood sheet ($1/2$-inch or $3/4$-inch thick)
- Four 1-inch by 4-inch boards for sides
- Saw
- Drill
- Wood screws
- Screwdriver
- Wood glue
- Large sheet of plastic for lining
- Two bricks
- 3-gallon plastic pail
- Sand or soil (sand preferred)
- Watering can

PROCEDURE:

1. Cut plywood into a rectangle the size you determine you want the stream table to be (for example, 2 feet by 5 feet). This will be the base.
2. Cut two 1-inch by 4-inch boards each the length of the long side of your plywood base plus 2 inches (for example, if your plywood is 5 feet long, you will cut 5 feet and 2 inches). These will be side pieces.
3. Cut two 1-inch by 4-inch boards each the length of the short side of your plywood base (for example, 2 feet). These will be front and back end pieces.
4. Secure the sides to the base with wood screws. First drill holes slightly smaller than the diameter of the screws, then insert the screws. Use wood glue on joints for added strength.
5. Secure the corners of the 1-inch by 4-inch side boards with wood screws.
6. Drill a ½-inch diameter hole through one of the shorter 1-inch by 4-inch end pieces just above the height at which it meets the plywood base. This will be the drain hole at the lower end of the stream table.

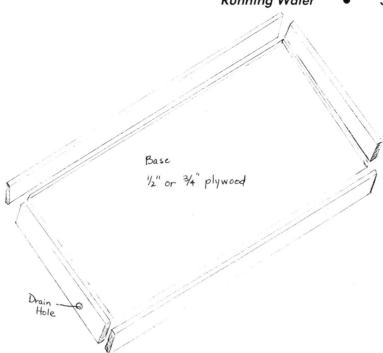

Base
½" or ¾" plywood

Drain Hole

Figure 6-1. Stream table construction.

7. Line the inside of the stream table with a piece of plastic large enough to cover the entire bottom area and extend up and over all four sides. (This could be an old shower curtain, a large garbage bag cut open to lie flat, or a roll of plastic sheeting purchased from a garden or hardware store.)

8. Punch a hole in the plastic lining at the spot where you drilled the hole in the stream table's end.

9. Place your stream table on a sturdy table or some other supporting surface so that it is high enough to position the pail under the drain hole in the end.

10. Elevate the upper end (no drain hole) of the stream table with a brick under each corner so the table slopes toward the drain.

11. Place the pail below the drain hole.

12. Put enough sand or soil in the stream table to cover the bottom to a depth of 2 to 3 inches.

    Note: The U.S. Army Corps of Engineers Waterways Experiment Station at Vicksburg, Mississippi, recommends using powderized coal. They have found it works best.

13. Clear sand from an area at the upper end of the stream table to provide a reservoir area.

14. Clear sand from an area at the lower end of the stream table (where drain hole is). This will be the lake that your river empties into.

15. Use a stick or your finger to make a small longitudinal channel in the center of the sand for the water to flow through.

16. Fill the watering can with water. Make sure it's less than the capacity of the pail at the stream table's outlet.

17. Slowly pour the water from the watering can into the reservoir at the upper end of the stream table.

18. Watch the water flow out of the reservoir into the channel.

Figure 6-2. Starting a channel in a stream table.

How does the flowing water change the shape of the channel you started with? How soon did a change start to occur? What happened to the channel by the time all the water passed through it?

• •

Erosion

Running water erodes the soil and rock it flows over, transports the eroded material, and deposits it in a new location. Erosion by flowing water takes three forms:

- Chemical reaction
- Hydraulic action
- Abrasion

Chemical Reaction

Chemical erosion occurs when water dissolves minerals in rock and soil and carries them downstream toward the sea. Both the resistance of the underlying rock and the solvent power of the water affect the rate of chemical erosion. Limestone is the most soluble of the major rock types. Granite and lava generally resist dissolving.

Water's solvent action increases with the absorption of carbon dioxide from the air to form carbonic acid. Dissolved organic acids from decaying vegetation also enhance water's solvent ability.

Chemical erosion is greater where water flows slowly than where water flows swiftly. The increased contact time between the water and the earth in slow-flowing areas allows more minerals to be dissolved.

A good example of water causing chemical erosion is acid rain. If acid rain falls on a susceptible rock like limestone, the rainwater dissolves the rock and carries minerals to streams where they are carried farther downstream.

Dissolved mineral salts aren't visible in water; they are carried as ions (electrically charged atomic particles). Scientists calculate that 3.85 billion net tons of dissolved material are transported by the world's rivers each year.

- The Niagara River alone carries away about 60 tons of dissolved minerals each minute.
- The city of Montreal, Quebec, is attempting to cut the amount of salt used to de-ice roads in the winter because the salt ends up in the Saint Lawrence River. This in turn alters the Saint Lawrence's salt balance and affects life in the river.

- One study found that the sixteen largest river systems in the world dump 56 tons of minerals into the oceans each second.
- Dissolved minerals and nutrients carried to the sea influence ocean life.

At one time it was thought that chemical erosion accounted for the oceans' mineral salt content. Now, however, we know more about under-sea volcanoes and lava flows, and we're not sure which is the more important source of sea salts—rivers or underwater volcanism.

Hydraulic Action

The force of running water widens cracks in the sides or bottoms of rivers so that portions eventually break off. This hydraulic action is more effective when the water flows swiftly.

Abrasion

Abrasion is the most powerful form of erosion caused by flowing water. Abrasion occurs when boulders, pebbles, and sand are picked up and moved by running water. They bounce along riverbeds and scour rivers' sides and bottoms like sandpaper on wood.

Faster-flowing water is more powerful and therefore more capable of causing abrasion. A fast-flowing river can carry boulders weighing many tons. Sound impossible? Just watch the news on television following a major flood. You may see cars or trucks being carried away by the tremendous force and volume of water. Entire bridges are sometimes washed away. When the speed of a river doubles like it often does during flooding, it far more than doubles its power to carry large, heavy objects.

■■■■■■■■■■■■■■■■■■■■■■■■■■■■■■■■■■■■■■

NIAGARA FALLS

Have you seen Niagara Falls? The Niagara River is geologically young, believed to be about twelve thousand years old. The cliff that creates Niagara Falls is capped with dolomite, a relatively erosion-resistant rock. The river undermines the dolomite cap through seepage as well as turbulence. Above the falls, water seeps through cracks in the dolomite and weakens the softer shale beneath it. Turbulent water at the base of the falls erodes the shale, and the undercut dolomite

Figure 6-3. Niagara Falls, New York. (New York State Department of Economic Development photograph)

above eventually gives way. It crumbles into small pieces or breaks off in enormous chunks.

Scientists estimate that during its long life the Niagara River's erosional activity has moved the site of the falls about 7 miles (11 kilometers) upstream, leaving the narrow gorge below. Until the 1950s the rate of Niagara Falls' retreat was from 3 to 6 feet (0.9 to 1.8 meters) annually. Since then, the rate has slowed because up to 75 percent of the river's water (150,000 cubic feet per second) is diverted above the falls into four large tunnels—two U.S. and two Canadian—to turn hydroelectric turbines generating 2,400 megawatts. That's enough electricity to light nearly 2 million homes.

Have you seen the Grand Canyon? It's about a mile (1.6 kilometers) deep. It was cut by the Colorado River, which is geologically about 5 to 6 million years old. Over its life the Colorado River has carved straight down to form the mile-deep canyon. The area's low rainfall, combined with the resistance of some of the rock layers, caused the canyon's walls to remain steep, with occasional rock terraces.

Think about the power and persistence of running water.

■■■■■■■■■■■■■■■■■■■■■■■■■■■■■■■■■■■■

Figure 6-4. Grand Canyon. (*National Park Service photograph.*)

Figure 6-5. Grand Canyon. (*National Park Service photograph by W. Belknap, Jr.*)

Transportation

We've already talked about how the world's rivers dissolve and carry billions of tons of mineral salts toward the sea every year. They also carry materials like clay, silt, and sand in suspension. In fact, rivers generally carry more material in suspension than in solution, which makes some rivers look muddy.

The Mississippi River carries more than 440 million tons of clay, silt, and sand annually. Because of this, its delta moves 6 miles (9.6 kilometers) seaward every hundred years. China's Huang He, or Yellow River (named for the color of the sediment), transports 1.6 billion tons of sediment annually. That's about 10 percent of the world's riverborne sediments. The Huang He sometimes looks like molasses as it carries this great sediment load toward the sea.

Three factors determine the amount of sediment a river will carry:

• Size of the sediments
• Volume of water in the river
• Velocity of the river

River *load* refers to the amount of sediment in the stream at a given time. A river whose sediments consist of large particles like pebbles and gravel will have a smaller load than will a comparable river with sand, silt, or clay sediment. *Competence* refers to the diameter of the largest particle a stream can transport. *Capacity* refers to the total amount of sediment a stream can transport.

Because clay particles are so small (less than $1/256$ millimeter in diameter), once suspended in running water they stay suspended. However, because of their strong cohesive properties, clay particles tend to clump together and stay together, making it tougher for a stream to dislodge them. When clumped together, clay acts like larger particles. Once dislodged, separated, and suspended, it remains suspended longer than larger-sized sediment particles.

When a river's volume (the amount of water it contains) increases, whether from precipitation or from tributary streams, its capacity also increases. There's simply more water available in which sediments may be suspended.

The ability of a stream to move sediments increases as its velocity increases. Velocity affects both a stream's competence and capacity.

Doubling the speed of a stream—during a flood, for instance—can increase its competence by as much as four times. That is, it can then move material four times larger than it could before. This is why very large and heavy items can be moved during floods. In a 1923 flood in the northwestern United States, for example, boulders as large as 90 tons were moved. Capacity also increases with increased stream velocity.

Rivers bear their highest concentrations of suspended material near their bottoms. Remember, too, that material too large for suspension is moved over the riverbed by being rolled or bounced along, significantly contributing to the river's abrasive ability. Researchers estimate that movement along the riverbed, or bed load, accounts for 7 to 10 percent of the river's total movement of material. In some cases, this figure can be as high as 50 percent.

Activity

Watch a nearby stream or river to see how it moves its load. Is the water muddy-looking, indicating a good deal of smaller suspended material? Is it a clear, rushing brook? Can you see pebbles rolling or bouncing along the bottom?

Activity

While you're at that stream or river, determine how fast it's flowing. Measure off a distance of 20 feet (about 6 meters) or more using a yardstick, tape measure, or your stride if you know its length.

Drop a stick, a piece of wood, or something else that floats (natural, please) into the center of the stream. Time how long it takes to cover the distance you measured. Divide the measured distance by the number of seconds it took the stick to travel the measured distance. This figure will be feet (or meters) per second. Convert that to miles (or kilometers) per hour.

Your answer will be surface flow speed. The speed in the stream's center below the surface will be different, as will the speed against the banks or near the bottom. Will the speed in these areas be slower or faster than the surface speed?

Deposition

The ultimate destination of rivers and any water flowing over land is the oceans. But rivers don't carry all their sediments all the way to the sea. They slow in spots and deposit some of their load. They flood and deposit sediment on their floodplains. They sometimes slow so much that they form deltas near their mouths. Once sediment settles out of a river or stream it is called *alluvium*. Hydrologists estimate that rivers deposit as much as 75 percent of their sediment load before reaching the sea.

● ●

PROJECT

Curving Streams

Have fun with your stream table. Watch how your river curves and see where it deposits alluvium.

MATERIALS:

- Stream table
- Water
- Watering can
- Pail

PROCEDURE:

1. Empty the pail beneath your stream table's drain if it's full.
2. Fill the watering can with water. You can reuse what was in the pail. Pour the water out of the pail slowly if there is any sediment settled on its bottom.
3. Slowly pour water from the watering can into the reservoir area at the top of the stream table and watch it flow through the channel.
4. Repeat this procedure several times until a definite curve or curves form in your "river."
5. Note where material is eroded and where sediment is deposited.

● ●

Figure 6-6. Meanders in a stream table.

How does the water flow around the curves, or *meanders,* of your stream? What happens to the banks along the outside of the curves? What about the inside banks?

Meanders

Although rivers flow toward the oceans, there are no straight rivers. It's even difficult to find a straight section of a river. That's because rivers tend to wander, or meander. Water chooses the path of least resistance. That means if something gets in its way, water just goes around it. Researchers have found that a straight channel section rarely exceeds a length equal to ten times the stream's width.

Nearly every stream has stretches of a meandering channel pattern. Even when there are no obstacles in a stream's path, it tends to form the looping curves known as meanders. Once it was thought that meandering resulted from the Coriolis effect produced by the earth's spinning on its axis. Modern research shows that this is not the case.

During the 1940s, the U.S. Waterways Experiment Station addressed the question of meanders. A series of small rivers was constructed, ranging from 1 to 5 feet wide and 50 to 150 feet long. These streams flowing over adjustable-height floors of sand and silt were like one huge stream table. At

| INITIAL STRAIGHT CHANNEL | AFTER 3 HOURS | AFTER 6 HOURS | AFTER 10 HOURS |

Figure 6-7. Classic modeling sequence showing how river meanders develop. (U.S. Army Corps of Engineers photograph)

the start, the stream channels were straight, but they soon began to change. A noticeable tendency to meander developed in three hours. In six hours the streams produced broad curves.

Further research into why a stream begins to curve led to the conclusion that meandering is a kind of energy-saving process for a river. Luna Leopold, a U.S. Geological Survey hydrologist, wrote in 1966, "Meanders are not mere accidents of nature but the form in which a river does the least work in turning, and hence are the most probable form a river can take."

Meanders commonly occur where a river crosses a gentle slope containing fine-grained, easily eroded material. As the stream enters a curve, the faster-moving water near its surface is forced against the outside or concave bank, thus eroding it. While the faster water takes the outside path, the slower water near the stream's bottom compensates by moving toward the inside or convex bank of the curve. Since sediment settles out of slower water more easily, it tends to deposit on the inside curves. As these processes build on each other, the meanders grow broader.

There is a limit to meanders, however. As it swings wider and wider, the curve becomes a loop that the river breaks through. The breakthrough is called a *cutoff*, and the abandoned meander eventually becomes an *oxbow lake*.

Braided Channels

When sediment load is too great to be supported by the volume and velocity of a stream, *braided* channels develop. Long, narrow, parallel sandbars separate the main channel into several smaller channels. The water often crosses from one channel to another, producing a braided appearance when seen from above. The Platte River in Nebraska has many braided channels.

Levees and Floodplains

When a great river overflows onto its *floodplain*—the level area along the river's bank that is submerged when the river floods—the water's velocity slows. The greatest slowing occurs just as the river dumps over its banks. More sediment leaves the water here than farther out on the floodplain. These thicker deposits form low ridges called *natural levees*.

As levees continue to build through successive floods, they can raise the elevation of the river to a greater height than the surrounding land. To control flooding, man sometimes builds levees or adds to natural levees.

Natural levees along the Mississippi River reach 16 feet (4.9 meters) in height. Some of the reinforced levees along the Mississippi River in Louisiana are 25 feet (7.6 meters) high. The city of New Orleans is now lower than the adjacent Mississippi River.

Back swamps and *yazoo streams* (streams parallel to the main river) may form on a river's floodplain beyond the levees. Flood plains, which are more common and broader along the lower (downstream) portions of rivers, contain some of the most fertile and tillable farmland in the world. New materials and nutrients borne by the water are added to the land here each time it floods. On the average, this occurs two out of every three years.

The Mississippi River's floodplain includes about 30,000 square miles of rich farmland from Cairo, Illinois, south to New Orleans, Louisiana. At its widest point, the Mississippi's floodplain measures 125 miles (201 kilometers).

Deltas

When a stream or river empties into a lake or ocean, it suddenly slows. The remaining sediment load is dumped there, nearly all at once. A *delta* will form at a river's mouth if the alluvium deposited there is able to avoid being carried away by the sea's currents and tides. Deltas may be triangular, fan-shaped, or bird's-foot shaped.

The Mississippi River delta is well known. Daily, the Mississippi adds about 1 million tons of alluvium to its delta area. In the last five thousand years, the Mississippi delta has added about 15,000 square miles of land to the state of Louisiana.

Deltas are important throughout the world—as are floodplains—because they are generally fertile areas where farming is a significant activity.

Other major world deltas include the Nile delta in Egypt, the Tigris and Euphrates delta in Iraq, the Niger delta in Nigeria, the Indus delta in Pakistan, the Amazon delta in Brazil, the Mekong delta in Vietnam, the Irrawaddy delta in Burma, and the Yangtze and Huang He deltas in China.

In the following activities, you can use your stream table to study different aspects of water flow just as hydrologists do.

● ●

PROJECT

Steepen That Slope

MATERIALS:

- Stream table
- Board or scraps of wood
- Water
- Watering can

PROCEDURE:

1. Raise the top end of your stream table another inch or two by adding a board or wood scraps to the bricks under that end.
2. Make sure the pail below the stream table's drain is empty.
3. Smooth out the sand (or soil or powdered coal) on the table and again make a starting channel with a stick or your finger.
4. Add water several times to the reservoir at the top of the stream table.
5. Watch what happens to the channel as water flows through it. How is it different from the channel formed when the table was sloped less? How is it similar? Why?
6. When you're finished, remove the extra board or wood scraps.

PROJECT

Obstacle Course

MATERIALS:

- Stream table
- Several small rocks or pebbles
- Water
- Watering can

PROCEDURE:

1. Make sure the pail below the stream table's drain is empty.
2. Smooth out the sand (or soil or powdered coal) on the table and again make a starting channel with a stick or your finger.

3. Add the rocks or pebbles to the channel bed you've made.
4. Add water to the reservoir at the top of the stream table.
5. Watch as your "river" encounters the obstacles you have placed in its path. How do they affect the course of the stream? Why?
6. When you're finished, remove the rocks or pebbles from the stream table.

PROJECT

Over the Falls

MATERIALS:

- Stream table
- Rock several inches wide and not quite as high as the sand on your stream table
- Water
- Watering can

PROCEDURE:

1. Make sure the pail below the stream table's drain is empty.
2. Smooth out the sand (or soil or powdered coal) on the table and make a shallow starting channel with a stick or your finger.
3. Bury the rock beneath the channel about two-thirds of the way down the channel.
4. Add water to the reservoir at the top of your stream table.
5. Watch what happens when the water erodes the channel bed to the level of the rock. You may need to add more water to the reservoir to keep the stream flowing.
6. When you're finished, remove the rock from the channel.

PROJECT

Floodplain and Levees

To get your "river" flowing slowly enough to overflow its banks onto a floodplain, you may need to remove the bricks that elevate the top end of the table and replace them with a board or wood scraps to get a very slight slope. *Note: If your stream table is very short, this experiment may not work well.*

MATERIALS:

- Stream table
- Water
- Watering can

PROCEDURE:

1. Make sure the pail below the stream table's drain is empty.
2. Smooth out the sand (or soil or powdered coal) on the table and make a shallow starting channel with a stick or your finger.
3. Add water to the reservoir at a rate great enough to encourage your "river" to overflow its banks. You may need to add water several times.
4. Watch for small levees building up along the river's banks. See what happens to the water on the floodplain. Does it form a swampy area? A yazoo stream?
5. Build up your own larger levees with sand from the table and make the river flow again.

PROJECT

Deltas

To get your "river" flowing slowly enough to form a delta, you may need to remove the bricks that elevate the top end of the table and replace them with a board or wood scraps to get a very slight slope.

Note: If your stream table is very short, this experiment may not work well.

MATERIALS:

- Stream table
- Water
- Watering can

PROCEDURE:

1. Make sure the pail below the stream table's drain is empty.
2. Smooth out the sand (or soil or powdered coal) on the table and make a shallow starting channel with a stick or your finger.
3. Add water to the reservoir to get the "river" flowing slowly. You may need to add water several times.

4. Watch for delta formation where the stream empties into the sea at the bottom of the stream table. What shape is the delta?

PROJECT

Shoreline Erosion

In this project, you don't need a channel, you simply need water in the lake at the lower end of the table.

MATERIALS:

- Stream table
- Cork or other plug to close drain hole
- Water
- Watering can
- Small, flat piece of wood
- Small rocks

PROCEDURE:

1. This time, after you smooth the sand (or soil or powdered coal), don't make a channel. Instead, enlarge the lake or sea at the lower end of the table.
2. Use the cork to plug the drain hole so water will not leave the lake or sea area.
3. Fill the lake area with water.
4. Float the small piece of wood on the water. Gently rock it enough to make waves against the shore of the lake.
5. Watch what the waves do to the shoreline.
6. How can erosion be prevented or slowed? Use sand or small rocks to build anti-erosion seawalls along the shoreline.
7. Make more waves and observe what happens to the shore.
8. Remove the rocks and build a breakwall just off the shore.
9. Make waves again and observe how the shoreline reacts.
10. Remove the breakwall and use the rocks to build a couple of short piers perpendicular to the shoreline.
11. Make waves again and observe how the shoreline reacts.
12. Remove the drain plug and drain the stream table.

● ●

Dams

In effect, dams block rivers to create artificial waterfalls. Today, dams tame many of the world's mighty rivers and produce an estimated 25 percent of the world's electricity.

When dams are mentioned, many people think of huge concrete structures. There are several methods of dam construction, including earthen embankments as well as concrete.

Activity

The next time you're at a small stream, look for accumulations of rock and debris that dam all or part of the stream. How is the water's flow affected?

Activity

There is probably some sort of dam or man-made flow restriction on a nearby river or stream—even the installation of a culvert into the flow of a stream or ditch beneath a road. Conservancy districts may administer river systems that include earthen dams. See what you can find out about the reasons for the flow alteration. You may be able to determine them, or you may want to contact your local or state government or conservancy head-quarters. How have changes by humans affected the surrounding area? How have they affected the river or stream itself?

Damming rivers is a controversial subject. The beneficial effects of dams include flood control, storage of water for dry periods, creation of lakes for fishing and recreational use, and production of electricity.

On the other hand, dams may move people from their homes, restrict the downstream water flow, endanger habitats of animals or plants, and disrupt the river's normal pattern of erosion and deposition. Water in a reservoir behind a dam moves slowly and dumps nearly all its sediments there. Water released by the dam is clearer than it otherwise would be and may cause renewed downstream erosion.

••

PROJECT

Dams

MATERIALS:

- Stream table
- Small board about 4 inches wide (Maybe you have a scrap of 1-inch by 4-inch board left from building your stream table.)
- Water
- Watering can

PROCEDURE:

1. Make sure the pail below the stream table's drain is empty.
2. Smooth out the sand (or soil or powdered coal) on the table and make a shallow starting channel with a stick or your finger.
3. Place the board into the sand and across the channel at some point to make a dam.
4. Add water to the reservoir at the top of the table so that the stream flows slowly.
5. Observe what happens both above and below the dam on your "river."
6. When you're finished, remove the board from the channel.

••

Complex changes in erosion and deposition resulted from construction of the Aswan High Dam in Egypt during the 1960s. Lake Nasser, the dam's 2,000-square-mile reservoir, robs the Nile floodplain and delta of the silt that formerly enriched these areas. Local farmers must now apply costly fertilizers to their land. The dam and reservoir also affected delta building at the Nile's mouth. Because less sediment arrives at the Nile delta, it is now losing ground to wave erosion by the Mediterranean Sea.

Recently, the high cost of large dams as well as environmental concerns have renewed interest in smaller dams and small-scale electrical power generation. Sometimes generating turbines are mounted in swiftly flowing streams with no dams. In other places, formerly abandoned small dams have been revitalized. Since 1968, more than ninety thousand small hydroelectric plants have been built in China.

■■■■■■■■■■■■■■■■■■■■■■■■■■■■■■■■■

DAMS AROUND THE WORLD

- The Syncrude Tailings Dam near Fort McMurray, Alberta, Canada, completed in 1992, contains 19 billion cubic feet (540 million cubic meters) of earth and rock fill. This makes it the world's most massive dam.

- 8.4 billion cubic feet (238,280,000 cubic meters) of earth and rock fill the Pati Dam on the Paraná River in Argentina. The dam is 108.6 miles (174.8 kilometers) long and 118 feet (36 meters) high.

- The Grand Coulee Dam on the Columbia River in Washington State is the world's largest concrete dam. It is 550 feet (168 meters) high and 4,173 feet (1,272 meters) long and contains 285 million cubic feet (80,703,014 cubic meters) of concrete. Currently it has the second greatest power generation capacity of any dam in the world—10,830 megawatts.

- Rogunskaya Dam on the Vakhsh River in Tadzhikstan is 1,098 feet (335 meters) high—the highest dam in the world. This earth-filled dam is 1,975 feet (602 meters) long.

- The world's second tallest dam is also on the Vakhsh River in Tadzhikstan. The Nurek Dam is 984 feet (300 meters) high.

- The Grande Dixence Dam on Switzerland's Dixence River ranks third highest in the world. It checks in at 932 feet (285 meters) tall.

- Canada's tallest dam is the Mica Dam on the Columbia River. It is 794 feet (242 meters) high.

- At 770 feet (235 meters) tall, the Oroville Dam on the Feather River in California is the highest dam in the United States.

- Glen Canyon Dam on the Colorado River in Arizona is 710 feet (216 meters) high and 1,560 feet (475 meters) long. It was completed in 1964 and ranks as the third-highest dam in the United States.

- Hoover Dam, on the Colorado River along the Arizona-Nevada border, was completed in 1936 and is 726 feet (221 meters) high and 4,173 feet (1,272 meters) long. Its reservoir, Lake Mead, covers 247 square miles (694 square kilometers).

- The world's largest man-made reservoir is the Bratskoye reservoir created by the Bratsk Dam on the Angara River in Siberia. Its volume is 40.6 cubic miles (169,270,000 cubic meters), and its surface area is 2,112 square miles (5,470 square kilometers).

- Close behind is Lake Nasser, formed by the Aswan High Dam across the Nile River in Egypt. It contains 21,988,290,800 cubic feet (168,900,000 cubic meters) of water and has a surface area of about 2,000 square miles (5,180 square kilometers).

• The reservoir of the Kariba Dam on the Zambezi River is 175 miles (282 kilometers) long and covers about 2,000 square miles (5,180 square kilometers). Completed in 1959, it is shared by Zimbabwe and Zambia.

• Lower Tunguska Dam on the Lower Tunguska River in the former Soviet Union will be the world's largest hydroelectric project in terms of electricity produced. The earth-filled dam is scheduled for completion in 1994. It will generate 20,000 megawatts.

• Currently, the Itaipu Dam on the Paraná River between Paraguay and Brazil generates the most electricity of any dam in the world—12,600 megawatts.

• Construction began in 1975 and was finished in 1983. The dam is 4.8 miles (7.7 kilometers) long and 62 stories high and creates an 870-square-mile (2,253 square kilometers) reservoir. Built at a cost of $13 billion, 15.7 million cubic yards (12 million cubic meters) of concrete were used in its construction, enough to build about eight medium-size cities. When its generators went on line in 1983 it was the world's largest hydroelectric installation.

■ ■

Perhaps the greatest river-alteration project of all time is La Grande Rivière, scheduled for completion in the year 2000. Located between Labrador and Quebec, the $15-billion project began in 1971. When finished, it will include 198 dikes, eight main dams, and five major reservoirs storing water for three power stations. The flow of three rivers will be channeled into the La Grande complex. The first generator went on line in 1979. When completed, the sixty turbines of its five main power stations will produce 13,900 megawatts—enough electricity for more than 10 million homes.

Who will use this electricity? The United States does not generate enough electricity to satisfy its demand, so it looks to other sources, like Canada. The province of Quebec, through La Grande Rivière, is helping meet U.S. power demands.

The La Grande project will affect the environment of 68,000 square miles (176,044 square kilometers), an area about the same size as the state of Washington, or almost 20,000 square miles (51,778 square kilometers) more than the size of New York State—where Quebec hopes to sell most of the electricity generated. The reservoir supplying the largest of the power stations covers 1,134 square miles (2,936 square kilometers)—about the size of the state of Rhode Island (1,045 square miles or 2,705 square kilometers). La Grande has stirred controversy as Native Inuit people and wildlife are driven from their land by the formation of new lakes. The Inuit had held the land for over a thousand years.

Endangered Rivers

Humankind's alterations to rivers bring both benefits and problems. These alterations also affect the rivers themselves, sometimes so much that a river's existence becomes endangered.

The Colorado River, with its tributaries, drains portions of seven states and is therefore important to the arid southwestern United States. Its flow is now controlled by ten major dams. Their associated power plants generate 12 million kilowatts of electricity needed by the western United States. The dams provide flood control as well as storage reservoirs for irrigation projects that have permitted arid areas like California's Imperial Valley to grow many food crops. Without the Colorado River, there would be no water for the cascading fountains adorning Las Vegas, Nevada, casinos. Without the Colorado, the water supply of San Diego, California, would be 10 percent less.

While these uses of the Colorado River resource are beneficial, the river itself suffers. By the time the Colorado River gets to the Gulf of California, it is reduced to a trickle. That's why some people call it our "most endangered river."

We face a challenge to use our water resources wisely.

■■■■■■■■■■■■■■■■■■■■■■■■■■■■■■■■■■■■■■■

WATERWAYS EXPERIMENT STATION

The U.S. Army Waterways Experiment Station (WES) was established by the U.S. Army Corps of Engineers in 1929. The facility's original mission was to test flood-control plans for the Mississippi River following a disastrous flood in 1927. The WES has expanded into a six-laboratory research, development, and testing complex located on a 685-acre reservation in Vicksburg, Mississippi. Its mission now is to develop and carry out engineering and scientific investigations to support the military and civil programs of the Corps of Engineers, the army, and the nation.

The Waterways Experiment Station's annual work-program budget is over $150 million and includes more than fifteen hundred projects for over 150 different sponsoring federal and state agencies.

Today there are over fifteen hundred civilian employees and several members of the armed forces assigned to the WES. Almost seven hundred are engineers and scientists specializing in areas such as hydraulics, oceanography, chemistry, electronics, computer science, ecology, physics, mathematics, soils, seismology, limnology, and microbiology.

Research proceeds in six separate but interrelated laboratories:

• *Hydraulics:* The Hydraulics Laboratory is the world's largest facility for research and practical application of experimental hydraulics. Scientists here use physical

Figure 6-8. The first hydraulic model at the Waterways Experiment Station for studying backwater on the Illinois River was carved from native soil about 1930. *(U.S. Army Corps of Engineers photograph)*

Figure 6-9. Technicians at WES use a probe to measure velocities on generalized outdoor research model. *(U.S. Army Corps of Engineers photograph)*

Figure 6-10. The WES New York Harbor model. *(U.S. Army Corps of Engineers photograph)*

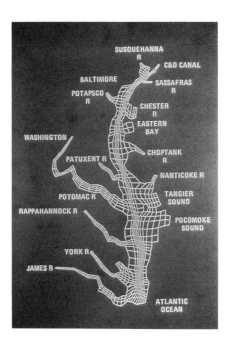

Figure 6-11. Physical models are being replaced and complemented with computer-driven numerical models, such as this computer-generated grid of the Chesapeake Bay system. *(U.S. Army Corps of Engineers photograph)*

models, computer-generated models, and field investigations relating to locks, levees, dredging, and channel realignments required for improved navigation and flood control in inland waterways. They also investigate shoaling, salinity, and navigation in tidal estuaries and examine the design and performance of hydraulic structures and reservoirs.

• *Coastal Engineering:* The Coastal Engineering Research Center gives us a better understanding of waves, currents, tides, winds, and other natural shoreline forces, as well as their interaction with beaches, inlets, the inner continental shelf, and man-made structures located within the coastal zone. Research focuses on problems relating to shore and beach erosion control, flooding and storm protection, coastal dredging, and coastal navigation channels and harbors.

• *Geotechnical:* The Geotechnical Laboratory researches human interaction with the earth's crustal materials—soil, rock, and groundwater. Information gained is useful in many aspects of the Corps of Engineers' responsibilities—dam and levee construction, pavements, earthquake engineering, and groundwater protection and contamination abatement.

• *Structures:* The Structures Laboratory examines the effects of nuclear and conventional weapons upon structures, determines ways to make concrete and other construction materials more durable, and investigates the behavior of natural and man-made structures under intense stresses.

• *Environmental:* The Environmental Laboratory experts study ecological interactions and environmental impacts in estuarine, marine, wetland, and freshwater areas. They are concerned with resource management, hazardous materials management, aquatic plant control, the environmental impact of dredging and dredged material disposal, environmental restoration, wetlands, water quality, and contaminated sediments.

• *Information Technology:* The Information Technology Laboratory has the task of information management at WES. Specialists here work with computer science, cartography, photographic documentation, illustration, publication, telecommunications, records management, printing, and library services.

Each year, approximately forty thousand people visit WES. Free guided tours of the facility are available to the public at 10 A.M. and 2 P.M., Monday through Friday (except national holidays). Self-guided tours are also available during regular working hours. For more information, contact:

U.S. Army Corps of Engineers
Waterways Experiment Station
Public Affairs Office
3909 Halls Ferry Road
Vicksburg, MS 39180–6199
(601) 634–2504

■■■■■■■■■■■■■■■■■■■■■■■■■■■■■■■■■■■■■■■

Chapter Seven

Getting Down and Dirty
•••
The Soil Beneath Your Feet

S oil. Dirt. It's a number of things to different people.
It's often the stuff your parents tell you to wipe off your feet before you come into your home. To a baby, it's something to pick up and put in her mouth. To a toddler, it's something to play in and squish between his fingers. You used to mix it with water and shape it into mud pies or other creations. The dog brings it in and leaves a pattern of footprints on the floor.

To a farmer, it means life for the crops—a farmer's livelihood depends upon the soil's fertility and moisture content. According to the *Dictionary of Geological Terms* (William H. Matthews, III, and Robert E. Boyer, American Geological Institute, 1976, Anchor Press/Doubleday), soil is "that earth material which has been so modified and acted upon by physical, chemical, and biological agents that it will support rooted plants. The term as used by engineers includes, in addition to the above, all *regolith*" (loose rock material above bedrock). To an earth scientist, it's a composite of loosely consolidated organic and inorganic materials generally found on or near the surface of the lithosphere.

Inside the house, soil is generally a nuisance, something to clean up. Outside, though, soil—or dirt—is an important, but unglamorous, resource. When natural resources are discussed, soil often gets left out. After all, it's just dirt.

But soil is important as a crossroads between the mineral and the organic worlds. As rock from the mineral world breaks into smaller particles through physical and chemical processes and combines with organic materials, it becomes soil.

The mineral and organic content of soil, together with the water and air in it, are essential to support plant life, which in turn supplies food for animal life. Soil type and fertility are key factors in determining the kinds of plant life it will support.

Some animal life depends directly upon the soil. Nearly 95 percent of all insects spend a part of their life cycle below ground. Other creatures, such as earthworms and burrowing animals, depend upon the earth to provide them with shelter.

Activity

Take a few minutes to go outside and pick up a handful of dirt. *Caution: To prevent possible contamination, make sure lawn chemicals, weed killers, or insecticides have not been used on the soil that you touch.* Is it dry? Wet? Slimy? How does it smell? Rub some between your fingers. Is it smooth? Gritty? Look at it carefully. Can you see individual soil particles? Do you see any organic matter like leaf shreds? Are any worms or insects visible? Think about your handful of dirt and how it was formed.

Soil Formation

Five factors affect soil formation: climate, parent material, topography, erosion, and biological activity.

Climate

An obvious way that climate affects soil is by determining the amount of water that enters the soil from precipitation. During a heavy downpour, most of the water runs off the land surface into sewers, drainage ditches, streams, or other bodies of water. On the other hand, a light, steady rain is more likely to soak into the soil and more efficiently increase its moisture content.

Likewise, a heavy snow cover that melts quickly produces a greater amount of runoff than does slowly melting snow. If it melts slowly, it adds more moisture to the soil below. Hail almost always adds moisture since it melts slowly after landing.

Rain that falls on and filters through the accumulation of organic matter on the ground picks up acids and minerals and carries them into soil in solution. This helps add minerals to the soil and can also set up a chain of complex chemical reactions. Calcium, potassium, sodium, and other mineral elements, and soluble salts and carbonates in solution are commonly carried deeper into the soil by percolating water. The greater the rainfall in an area, the more water moves downward through the soil and the less it moves upward. In desert regions, the opposite is true.

Besides determining how fast snow and hail melt, daily temperature helps determine how much precipitation evaporates before it can penetrate the ground. Temperature also regulates the speed of chemical reactions in the soil and influences plant growth.

Parent Material

A major portion of soil is mineral matter, which is supplied by the soil's parent material. Parent material is also the fundamental influence on soil texture—the mix of different-size particles composing soil. Texture determines the pore size of the soil, which in turn determines both the amount of water the soil can hold and the gases present in the soil.

You can think of it in terms of physical characteristics that you inherited from your parents—general body size, skin color, hair color and texture, eye color. In this case, the soil's characteristics can be traced back to similar qualities in its ancestry.

The source of soil's parent material is bedrock—the solid rock that underlies loose material on the ground. Upper portions of bedrock break apart through physical or chemical processes to become parent material, or regolith. Regolith adds highly weather-resistant minerals such as quartz to the soil. Because parent material is mineral matter, it contributes a majority of the soil's mineral content. Feldspar in parent material yields primary soil minerals such as aluminum and silicon. Iron compounds in the parent material oxidize to their red ferric states or reduce to their gray-colored ferrous states in the soil. Parent material, therefore, also contributes to the soil's color.

Topography

Topography—the shape of the land surface—influences soil primarily by controlling water movement over and within the soil. In any location, the slope of the land determines how fast and in what direction water will flow across the surface as well as through the soil.

Activity

An area's drainage is dependent upon its topography. You can see this for yourself on a small scale in your yard or a nearby park or construction site. Go there immediately following a heavy rainfall (as long as it's not a flood) and look at the ground, especially where soil is visible. Is there any standing water? Where does it collect? Which way does it flow? Why?

In low-lying areas, water can accumulate and the soil may become waterlogged, while higher areas may become dry. This in turn affects the biological community within the soil. Topography also affects stream flow speed. Across steeper topography, streams flow swiftly. Where the grade is gentle or nearly level, streams flow sluggishly. In more level areas, sediment may accumulate along stream banks and contribute fertile, *alluvial* (deposited by water) soil to the area.

Erosion

Erosion is the removal of soil by running water or wind. Humans can accelerate erosion in an area by the removal of vegetation. We can also act as erosional agents by transporting soil from one place to another with heavy equipment. If the rate of erosion is greater than the rate of soil formation, the soil will eventually disappear. If erosion can be slowed or stopped, new soil will be able to build up.

Vegetation is an important factor in slowing erosion and preserving the soil. Vegetation holds soil particles in place so running water and wind cannot carry them away. Soil-smart farming practices like contour plowing, terracing, and cover cropping also preserve soil.

Biological Activity

Because of the varied biological activity in it, soil is a living, dynamic substance rather than just an accumulation of sterile rock particles and minerals.

Biological activity includes growth and decay of plants and animals in the soil and above the soil. It includes the activities of earthworms and other soil-dwelling animals, bacteria, and fungi. This biological activity adds organic matter, or *humus,* to the soil. And organic matter is the basic storage container for nutrients needed by the area's ecosystem. For example, through photosynthesis, plants add a portion of the sun's energy to the soil as organic carbon. Worldwide, this adds approximately 18 billion metric tons of carbon to soil each year.

Soil's biological activity also produces organic acids that help break down the parent rock material. Do you know any farmers or serious gardeners? They measure their soil's *pH* (hydrogen ion concentration, a measure of acidity) to help determine what types of crops to grow or to make sure it is within the range suited to the plants they want to grow. What isn't widely known is that the acidity produced by biological activity acts upon rock particles in and beneath the soil to dissolve minerals and help break down the rock particles.

Plant roots and burrowing animals penetrate to various depths and directions beneath the soil's surface. This aerates the soil and creates pathways for water distribution within the soil. "Good" soils—good for plant life—have 40 to 60 percent of their bulk occupied by pore space. Much of this pore space results from biological activity. The pore space may be filled with either water or air, both of which are important to plants.

Vegetation itself helps regulate water losses from evapotranspiration and protects the soil from excessive erosion by holding soil particles during water runoff. Vegetation type is also important in determining soil characteristics such as organic and nutrient content, and color. For example, the thick grass cover of the native American prairies helped develop a different type of soil than developed in originally forested areas.

So biological activity influences a variety of aspects of soil, from soil formation to its ability to support life.

Soil Horizons

Soil horizons are separate soil layers with distinct characteristics. They develop as soil forms above the bedrock and are identified by soil scientists with the letters *A*, *B*, *C*, and sometimes *O*.

● ●

PROJECT

Soil Layers

To see the different layers of the soil, you can dig a sample from your yard or look at a nearby cliff or road cut.

MATERIALS:

- Soil sampler, post-hole digger (clam-shell type), or narrow spade
- Several thicknesses of newspaper
- A place to dig

PROCEDURE:

1. If you can't find a place from which to *safely* observe the soil and rock layers of a cliff or road cut, choose a spot where you can dig a hole.
2. Use a soil sampler to extract a narrow cylinder of soil. If you're using a spade or post-hole digger, dig a small-diameter hole at a slight angle so that you can lift the soil without disturbing it.
3. Place the soil sample carefully onto the newspaper.
4. Try to dig deeper into the same hole to get a second sample from deeper down.
5. Place the second sample on the newspaper in line with and below the first.
6. How many different layers of soil can you identify? Two or three?

● ●

A cross section of soil horizons is called a *soil profile*; it shows the different layers of a particular soil.

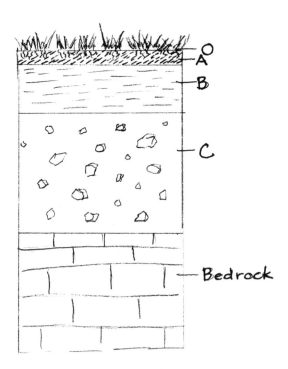

Figure 7-1. Typical soil profile.

The uppermost layer of a soil profile is the *A horizon*. It can be less than an inch to many feet thick. Much of the biological activity in soil goes on in this layer. Earthworm, beetle, and bacterial activity constantly makes new soil by decomposing organic matter and breaking apart larger pieces of soil. *Topsoil* is in the A horizon. Topsoil is made up mainly of humus and other organic material provided by plants and small soil animals.

■■

It takes perhaps five hundred years for an inch of soil to form, but humans, armed with destructive farming practices (like monocropping, not cover cropping or contour plowing) can destroy an inch of the A horizon, the most life-supporting layer, in only a few years. It has been estimated that in about two hundred years of farming in the United States, over 60 percent of the topsoil has been destroyed.

■■

The *B horizon* lies directly below the A horizon. It is often referred to as *subsoil*. Generally, the B horizon contains a concentration of iron and aluminum compounds, clay, and humus. Lighter in color than the topsoil, it is often somewhat compacted and firmer than the A horizon. The B horizon may have granular, blocky, or prismatic structures present. This horizon may be absent in some soils.

The *C horizon* consists of partly weathered rock material that may be either the same as or different from the material from which the A and B horizons above were formed. It is parent material that has already begun the process of becoming soil. The C horizon extends downward as far as the top of the unweathered rock, or bedrock.

Some scientists label an *O horizon* above the A horizon. The O horizon refers to the surface layer formed or in the process of forming above the other mineral-rich layers. It is composed of fresh or partially decomposed organic material.

Soil that has developed A, B, and C horizons is called a *mature soil*. On the other hand, soil that contains only two of the three horizons is referred to as an *immature soil*.

Chapter Eight

The Dirty Truth
•••

Sand, Silt, or Clay?

When your mom or dad warns you, "Don't come in until you take off those muddy shoes," it's all dirt to them. They don't care about the different soil-size classifications. But take a look at the stuff clinging to your shoes. Can you see individual particles or does it just look like a solid mass?

Soil comes in three basic particle sizes: sand, silt, and clay. The largest-size soil particles are sand; medium-size particles are silt; the smallest particles are clay. Sand may also be broken down into categories of very coarse, coarse, medium, fine, and very fine.

Some sources may call the middle size *loam*. Loam, however, is a soil type composed of a mixture of clay, silt, sand, and organic matter. Other sources may include gravel as the largest-size soil particle—larger than sand. But gravel doesn't always behave as soil. Since gravel particles include anything over 2 millimeters in diameter, most gravel is really too large to be called soil. Loam and gravel, however, are listed in Table 8-1 to help you sort things out and eliminate confusion.

The size of the particles making up soil determines its *texture*. Coarse-textured soils are made up of larger-sized particles than are medium- or fine-textured soils. Soils with fine texture are composed of the smallest particles.

Table 8-1. SOIL PARTICLE SIZE

Clay:	Less than $1/256$ mm diameter
Silt:	$1/256$ mm to $1/16$ mm diameter
Sand:	$1/16$ mm to 2 mm diameter
Very Coarse	1 mm to 2 mm diameter
Coarse	$1/2$ mm to 1 mm diameter
Medium	$1/4$ mm to $1/2$ mm diameter
Fine	$1/8$ mm to $1/4$ mm diameter
Very Fine	$1/16$ mm to $1/8$ mm diameter
Loam:	A soil composed of a mixture of clay, silt, sand, and organic matter
Gravel:	Greater than 2 mm diameter
Boulder Gravel	Greater than 256 mm diameter
Cobble	64 mm to 256 mm diameter
Pebble	2 mm to 64 mm diameter

Think of your muddy shoes again. As far as your parents are concerned, dirt is dirt. But to the soil scientist, the construction engineer, or the farmer, soil texture is important.

You may remember from the previous chapter that a "good" quality soil has 40 to 60 percent of its bulk, or volume, occupied by pore space. And pore space is determined by how small or large the individual soil particles are. Pore space, in turn, is one factor affecting soil drainage. Water quickly drains through the pore spaces of sandy soil but tends to puddle on the surface of clay soil, where the smaller individual particles pack together more tightly.

Ideally, gardeners and farmers want soil that drains well but doesn't dry out too quickly, has plenty of pore space for aeration of plant roots, and is fertile—that is, it holds nutrients that are readily available to the plants. Experts say that a good soil for plant life is a mixture of 40 percent silt, 40 percent sand, and 20 percent clay.

What type or mixture do you think would be desirable for an outdoor sports stadium?

Activity

That dirt on your shoes—how can you tell whether it is silt, sand, or clay?

Look at it carefully. Most likely it is a mixture of particle sizes. With your eyes alone, you should be able to see individual very coarse and coarse sand particles. If you use a 10X hand lens (it magnifies ten times), you will be able to see the various sizes of sand particles. At diameters of $1/16$ to $1/256$ millimeter, silt particles are virtually impossible to see even with a 10X hand lens. Clay particles, less than $1/256$ millimeter in diameter, are visible only with the aid of a microscope.

To get an idea of just how small soil particles can be, look at a metric ruler. The smallest marks are millimeters. There are a thousand of them in each meter. It takes more than 256 individual clay particles side by side to stretch the distance of 1 millimeter.

Activity

You can get a rough idea of the texture of the dirt on your shoes, or any sample of soil, by moistening it (if it isn't damp already) and rubbing a small amount between your fingers.

If the soil is coarse and gritty to the touch, falls apart when moist, and easily reveals separate particles or grains, the soil is considered sandy.

When moist silt is rubbed between your fingers it will become rough and broken. It may leave a slight smear on your hand.

Clay soils are very sticky and plastic when wet, almost like modeling clay. In fact, potter's clays are refined from soils with an extremely high clay content. When clay soils are dry, they form hard clumps and are very difficult to crush by hand. When moist and rubbed between your finger, clay soils feel smooth and make a continuous smear.

Soil Sampling

Since you need to dig a hole to remove a sample of soil, get permission first. If you're taking it from your yard, check with your parents and then take it from an isolated spot—perhaps a corner of the garden, the back of a flower bed, or the edge of the lawn. Offer to replace the sample when you're done and restore the surface. If you don't have a yard of your own, check with a friend or relative who does. Perhaps there's a nearby field or undeveloped lot that you could obtain a small sample from.

Caution: To prevent possible contamination, make sure lawn chemicals, weed killers, or insecticides have not been used on the soil that you touch.

When taking a soil sample, remember that it's best to have a representative sample of your entire area. If possible, take several small samples from three widely separated spots. The best time to gather soil samples is on a fairly dry day.

Taking a Soil Sample

- Pull or scrape aside leaves, grass, or other organic matter so that no mulch or decaying material is included in the sample.
- Dig down about 6 inches (15 centimeters) if you can so the sample contains dirt from the surface down to that depth.
- Place your samplings into a clean pail—plastic, if possible—so that no foreign elements like rust get into the soil. Thoroughly mix the soil in the pail.

In the following projects, you do not need to see the separate soil particles, but you will be able to determine the relative composition as well as other characteristics of the soil you sample. To see how soil varies from one part of a community to another, from one area of the country to another, or even from your back yard to your front yard, repeat the following projects with soil samples from other places. Then, if you have some commercially prepared and packaged soil (potting soil or topsoil), try the experiments with it.

• •

PROJECT

Mud Balls

Here's your chance to play in the dirt and make mud pies—well actually, mud balls. This project will demonstrate the general particle size of your soil samples.

MATERIALS:

- Small shovel or trowel
- Plastic pail, large plastic container, or 2-pound coffee can (or can of similar size)
- Plastic spoon
- Water

PROCEDURE:

1. Collect soil from different parts of your yard or other area as directed in the previous section, "Taking a Soil Sample," or use purchased potting soil if no other soil is available.
2. Place the soil in the container and mix well.
3. Put a heaping spoonful of the soil in your hand and add water, a few drops at a time, until the soil can be rolled into a ball. (If you use too much water and get a slurry, take another spoonful of dirt and try again.)
4. Let the ball of soil lie in your open hand and observe how your "mud ball" does or doesn't stay together. What size soil particle appears to make up most of the mud ball?
   a. If it's mostly clay, it will stay in a ball shape.
   b. If it's mostly silt, some soil will fall off the ball.
   c. If it's mostly sand, the ball will fall apart.

How does soil particle size affect the tendency of soil to clump together?

Try this project in different parts of your town or city, or in other areas of the country if you travel. This is a quick way to tell soil texture and particle size.

PROJECT

Dividing the Dirt

Making mud balls is fun, but you probably noticed in the previous project that your mud ball didn't behave completely like any of the descriptions of sand, silt, or clay. Most likely, it fell somewhere in between. That means your soil sample contains a variety of different-size particles.

Here is an easy way to separate the particles by size so you can see the proportions of sand, silt, and clay in the soil. Again, you may want to try this with more than one soil sample.

MATERIALS:

- Soil sample
- Clear glass or plastic jar with tight-fitting lid
- Water

PROCEDURE:

1. Fill jar half full with soil.
2. Add water to the jar until it's about ³/₄ full of soil and water.
3. Put the lid on the jar tightly.
4. Agitate—shake the jar.
5. Let the jar stand overnight to allow its contents to settle.
6. Carefully examine the jar's contents without disturbing them. What does the soil look like now? How has it settled? Is the soil in layers? What can you tell about the different layers of soil in the bottom of the jar?

    When you compared the soil layers, you probably noticed that the particles on the bottom are larger. They get smaller as you move toward the top of the soil in the jar. Sand particles will be on the bottom. Being the largest and heaviest, they settle first. Silt particles—in the middle in size and weight—settle out next and appear in the middle. Finally, the very small and light clay particles will be the top layer of the soil in the jar.
7. Measure the approximate heights of the layers. Using the total height of the soil in the jar, figure out what the percentages are of sand, silt, and clay in your sample. How does it compare to "good" garden soil (40 percent sand, 40 percent silt, 20 percent clay)?

• •

Pore Space: Just a Bunch of Air

The earth feels solid beneath your feet, doesn't it? But the dirt you're standing on isn't solid. Soil contains open space filled with air, or *pore space*. Some soils contain more; others contain less. Pore space affects drainage and provides air to plant roots. Other things being equal, a perfect garden soil should contain about 25 percent pore space by volume.

• •

PROJECT

Pore Space

MATERIALS:

- Two clear jars or beakers marked at 10-milliliter intervals to the 100-milliliter level
- Soil sample
- Water

PROCEDURE:

1. *Note: Use dry soil.* Fill one of the jars or beakers to the 100-milliliter mark with soil from your sample.
2. Fill the second jar or beaker to the 100-milliliter mark with water.
3. *Slowly* pour water from the second jar or beaker into the first until the water reaches the level of the top of the soil.
4. How much pore space was in the soil? Calculate the volume of water that you added to the soil. (Subtract the amount remaining in the second jar or beaker from the original amount—100 milliliters.) This is the volume of the pore space in the soil.

For Further Investigation:
- Try this procedure again using commercial potting soil. Which has more pore space—your soil or potting soil? Why does potting soil have the amount of pore space it does? Remember that many experts believe that the perfect garden soil has about 25 percent pore space.

• •

Permeability and Retentivity

Two other important soil characteristics affected by pore space are *permeability* (the capacity for transmitting a fluid, such as water) and *retentivity* (the tendency to retain a fluid). These two factors go hand in hand. When a fluid is added to soil—when you water plants in flowerpots or when rain falls on the earth—some will pass through because of permeability, and the rest will remain in the soil because of its retentivity.

PROJECT

Does It Just Pass Through or Stay for a While?

MATERIALS:

- Soil
- Aluminum pie pan
- Oven
- Plastic tube, 2 feet (0.6 meters) or less in length and less than 1 inch (2.54 centimeters) in diameter, open at both ends
- Square of soft cloth
- Rubber band
- 100-milliliter graduated cylinder
- Balance
- Beaker of more than 100-milliliter capacity
- Water
- Stand, optional
- Stopwatch or watch with second hand
- Paper and pencil

PROCEDURE:

1. Dry the soil by placing it in the aluminum pie pan. Put the pan in an oven turned on to its lowest heat setting. Check the soil at two-minute intervals until it is dry. The time it takes to dry will depend upon how wet it is initially as well as the oven temperature.

    Caution: Use hot pads when inserting and removing the pie pan from the oven. Ask an adult for permission to use the oven as well as instructions on how to use it if you aren't sure.

    Note: Soil drying in an oven may cause an unpleasant or offensive odor because of the soil's organic or humus content. Ventilate the area when drying soil.

2. Use the balance to weigh the empty tube, piece of cloth, and rubber band. Record their total weight.

3. Use the rubber band to secure the cloth over one end of the plastic tube.

4. Fill the tube half full with dry soil.

5. Weigh the tube with soil and record the weight.

6. Calculate the weight of the soil in the tube. (Subtract the weight of the empty tube, cloth, and rubber band determined in step 2 from the weight of the tube with soil.)

7. Hold the tube vertically, cloth-covered end down. (If you have a stand, fasten the tube to it.) Place the beaker under the tube.

8. Pour 100 milliliters of water into the soil in the tube.

9. How much time passes between pouring the water onto the soil and the first drop of water coming through the cloth into the beaker? Record the elapsed time.

10. When water stops dripping from the tube, measure the amount in the beaker. What does this tell you about the soil sample's permeability? You could express this as volume per period of time, such as 1 milliliter per second.

11. How much water did your soil sample retain? *Hint*: Subtract the volume of water that passed through the soil from the volume of water poured onto the soil sample (100 milliliters). 100 ml − __ ml (passing through) = __ ml retained. Retentivity is expressed as the weight of water retained per weight of dry soil. Since pure, fresh water weighs 1 gram per cubic centimeter (cc) at 4° Celsius (or 62.4 pounds per cubic foot), you can determine retentivity of your soil sample. Remember that 1 ml = 1 cc. For your information: Seawater ranges from 1.026 to 1.028 grams per cubic centimeter.

What quality of soil do you think determines permeability and retentivity? How do you think texture affects permeability and retentivity? You may want to repeat this experiment with sandy soil or beach sand as well as with clay soil or potter's clay.

● ●

Permeability and retentivity of soil are primarily determined by its texture. Coarse-textured soils—that is, soils with larger particles—have low capacities to store water. Most of the water that falls on them passes through, or permeates, the soil.

Soil that is mostly clay can retain large volumes of water in the upper part of the soil's profile. On the other hand, little water passes through clay soil, meaning its permeability is low. This is why clay soils tend to be poorly drained, particularly in flatter areas. Clay soils easily become waterlogged, preventing air from reaching plant roots.

Soil or gardening consultants perform some of the same soil evaluations that you've done. Often they can tell the suitability of the soil for gardening, farming, a sports field, or another use just by looking at several handfuls of soil.

You can be a soil detective, too. If your soil doesn't seem right for gardening or for that baseball diamond, what can be done to improve it for that use? Think about drainage, texture, retentivity. What will happen during a heavy rainfall?

For Further Investigation:

- What is the relationship between permeability and retentivity? Can it be mathematically expressed?
- According to the experts, a "perfect" garden soil contains about 25 percent water. What soil qualities do you think would be desirable for an area to be used as a sports field?
- As you collect soil samples from different areas, keep a notebook in which you list facts about the areas from which you took the samples. Record things like types of plants growing there. Certain types of plants like sandy soil; others may prefer silt or clay soil. Is there any standing water? How does the drainage appear?
- If you're in a city or suburban area, zoning is affected by soil type. Your city hall will have a zoning map; ask to see one. You may also check with the city engineer for a soil map of the city.
- Where would you locate a house with a basement? In a soil that is mainly clay or mainly sand? Remember that rainwater or melting snow will tend to stay on the ground and in the upper layers of soil around your house if it's built in clay soil. What could you do to improve drainage?

Discovering what's beneath your feet in your community goes beyond coming home with muddy shoes.

Chapter Nine

Will It Support Life?

Biological Components of Soil

Biologic activity is one of the five factors that affect soil formation. It includes small animals that burrow into the soil as well as *humus*—small particles of organic matter like leaves and grass decaying in the soil—and the microscopic organisms that aid in its decomposition.

Remember the mud on your shoes? There probably aren't earthworms or other visible animals in it. But chances are that bits of humus as well as microscopic creatures are present.

Biologic soil activity also includes the plants that are anchored in the soil and derive nutrients from it. Plants ranging from the tallest, oldest trees to the tiniest, most delicate alpine plants need soil to live. The plants draw nutrients—minerals and other chemicals—from the soil and depend upon the soil as an anchorage for their roots. In turn, plant roots help aerate soil and hold it in place in the face of erosion.

If you've observed the various locations where you may have gathered soil samples, you probably noticed that certain plants preferred certain locations. Several factors affect plants' preferences, including topography, climate, soil type and texture, and soil fertility. While all these conditions are important, no plant can survive if the soil around its roots lacks the necessary nutrients. *Soil fertility* can be defined as the ability of a soil to supply essential nutrients to plants. This ability depends on both the chemical and textural properties of the soil.

81

Humus

The presence of humus affects soil fertility, since the decay of organic matter provides plant nutrition by releasing certain chemicals in a form that plants can use. Remember, the "perfect" soil isn't solid dirt. Ideally, it contains 25 percent water and 25 percent pore space. It also contains organic matter, or humus.

Organic matter has been called "the storehouse of the soil's nutrients." It is vital to soil because

- it improves tilth and structure,
- it improves water-holding capacity,
- it aids in nitrogen fixation, and
- it makes nutrients available to plants.

Wesley Chaffin and Robert Woodward, agronomists at Oklahoma A & M College, wrote: "Nearly all of the nitrogen and sulfur, and more than one-third of the phosphorus that become available for plant use are supplied by the organic matter. Smaller quantities of the other plant nutrients also come from this source. Consequently, an increase in the rate of organic matter decomposition likewise increases the quantities of nitrogen, phosphorus, potassium, calcium, magnesium, and other plant nutrients in the soil solution."

● ●

PROJECT

How Much Humus?

This project will help you determine how much organic matter is in a sample of soil. However, the process may produce an offensive odor as the organic or humus content of the soil you are heating burns away, so check with an adult beforehand and do it outdoors.

Caution: Wear gloves and use hot pads or tongs when placing can on and removing can from the stove. Ask an adult for permission to use the propane stove as well as instructions on how to use it if you aren't sure. Propane combustion produces potentially harmful gases. Use the stove outdoors.

MATERIALS:

- Dry soil sample
- Empty soup can (15-ounce/425-gram size) with label removed
- Propane camp stove

- Heatproof surface
- Tongs or hot pads to grasp hot can
- Gloves
- Safety glasses
- Balance
- Small piece of paper or leaf

PROCEDURE:

1. Weigh the empty can with label removed.
2. Fill the can to near the top with dry soil. *Caution: Be sure the soil does not contain rocks, stones, or pebbles because they may explode when heated.*
3. Weigh the can with soil in it.
4. Calculate the weight of the soil alone.
5. Place a small piece of paper or dry leaf on top of the soil. *Caution: Wear gloves and safety glasses for the following steps.*
6. Turn on one stove burner according to manufacturer's instructions. Put the can of soil on the burner and heat until the paper or leaf turns to ash. *Note: The odor given off may be offensive. Perform outdoors.*
7. Turn stove off. Wearing gloves and using tongs or hot pads, remove can to heatproof surface and let can and soil cool.
8. Weigh can and soil again.
9. How much humus was burned off? (Subtract weight of heated can and soil from weight of can and soil before heating determined in step 3.)
10. Divide the weight of humus (from step 9) by the original weight of the soil (from step 4). Multiply by one hundred to get the percentage of the soil sample that is organic matter.

How does your sample compare to the "perfect" garden soil that is 5 percent humus?

• •

Minerals

To support healthy plant life, soil must also contain mineral elements such as iron, copper, manganese, calcium, zinc, molybdenum, and cobalt. Without elaborate testing equipment, we can't test the presence of these individual elements. We can, however, look for life in the soil. An abundance of life suggests that the soil probably contains necessary minerals.

The presence of certain plants also indicates the presence of certain elements. For example, a garden where beets do very well has soil that contains boron, since beets need boron and are sensitive to low or absent boron in soil. (The soil also has the proper tilth, or texture, allowing root crops like beets to expand.)

By the way, a "perfect" garden soil is 45 percent minerals. Sounds like a lot, doesn't it? But it's not surprising when you remember that soil's parent material—the bits of weathered and broken rock that form the basis for soil—are composed of minerals.

• •

PROJECT

What Life Lurks Beneath Your Feet?

Don't look to the mud on your shoes to show much life, although it may get a lively response from your parents. To find soil life, you'll need to gather fresh soil from an area that hasn't been treated with lawn chemicals or garden fertilizers and pesticides. Such products can kill or drastically reduce the living things in soil. They can also be harmful if they get on your skin.

MATERIALS:

- Small garden shovel
- Clean, empty coffee can or other container
- Aluminum pie pan or pizza pan
- 10X hand lens
- Tweezers

PROCEDURE:

1. Find a spot in your yard (or other land where you have permission to dig) that has not been treated with lawn or garden chemicals.
2. Dig soil from the top few inches and place it in your coffee can or pail.
3. Pour some soil into the aluminum pan and spread it out to cover the bottom of the pan.
4. Use the tweezers and 10X hand lens to look carefully through the soil in the pan to find living things.

5. Repeat steps 3 and 4 with the rest of your soil sample.

6. You may want to record what you find.

Examples of animals you may find include earthworms, night crawlers, insect larvae, maggots, caterpillars, slugs, snails, spiders, mites, ticks, ants, and other insects. Under the powerful magnification of a microscope, you might be able to see smaller life-forms.

Obtain fresh soil samples from different locations and compare the types and amount of living things you find.

• •

Acid or Alkaline: The pH Factor

The acid-alkaline balance, or *pH,* of soil is important for two reasons. First, it determines whether rock will be broken down to form soil. Certain minerals in rock are more sensitive to acids than are others. Acids moving downward through the soil profile can attack vulnerable minerals in the rock below, dissolving some, leaving resistant ones intact, forming new compounds, and breaking the rock into smaller pieces.

Second, acidity and alkalinity are important in the chemical formation of plant nutrients. A neutral to slightly acid soil offers the most favorable environment for the soil microorganisms that convert nitrogen from the air to a form available to plants. It also provides the best environment for the bacteria that decompose plant tissue to form humus. In this neutral to slightly acid pH range, all of the essential mineral nutrients are available to plants in sufficient quantities, and generally in a greater amount than at any other pH. Also, soil having a pH in this range is usually easily cultivated.

pH Scale

The pH scale expresses a substance's hydrogen ion concentration, which determines the acidity or alkalinity of that substance. Think of the pH scale as sort of an acid-alkaline meter. The scale is divided into points running from 0 to 14. The neutral point is 7, with numbers less than 7 representing increasing acidity and numbers greater than 7 increasing alkalinity. This doesn't mean, however, that neutral soil is neither acid nor alkaline (also called base), but rather that the two conditions are exactly balanced. A balanced condition means that the nourishment present in the soil is unlocked and ready to give plants the vitality necessary to grow, produce, multiply, and resist disease.

• •

PROJECT

pH Test

Note: Make sure your collecting shovel and container are clean and dry. Do not touch the soil sample with your hands.

MATERIALS:

- Soil sample from top 3 inches. *Note: Do not use wet soil.*
- pH testing kit (available from farm and garden stores or science supply catalog)
- Glass jar or beaker
- Distilled water (Tap water may not be pH neutral.)

PROCEDURE:

1. Mix an equal amount of soil and distilled water in the glass container. Stir or shake to mix well.
2. Let the mixture settle until liquid is clear.
3. Dip a pH test strip into liquid and remove. Wait thirty seconds.
4. Compare the color of the test strip with a color chart or other device supplied with the test kit.

• •

Activity

If you're able to check the pH of soil from different locations, note what kinds of plants thrive in different pH ranges. Here are some examples:

    pH 6.0–8.0 Trees: buckeye, ash, cherry
               Garden crops: peas, beans, squash
    pH 6.0–6.9 Most garden and field crops
    pH 5.0–6.0 Trees: apple, spruce
               Garden crops: strawberries
    pH 4.0–5.0 Trees: mountain ash, white cedar
               Flowering shrubs: azalea, rhododendron
               Plants: Venus flytrap

Correcting Acid-Alkaline Balance

If soil is too acidic, it may be corrected by the addition of crushed limestone or dolomitic limestone. (Dolomite contains some magnesium, which is essential for plant nutrition, and soil is often magnesium deficient.) Wood ashes and ground oyster shells may also be used to balance soil that is too acidic.

It's best to add just a little at a time. Just like adding salt to the soup, it's easier to start with a little and gradually add more than to try to remove excess. Lime may have to be added to soil every three years.

Organic matter will improve soil that is too alkaline. Even in large quantities it won't hurt the soil; in fact, it will only help. Organic matter contains natural acid-forming materials that produce acids on decomposition. The acids combine with excess alkali to neutralize it. Other additions that correct alkalinity are organic fertilizers with a low pH such as cottonseed meal and acid peat.

N, P, and K: Major Nutrients

Both chemical and natural lawn and garden fertilizers are labeled according to the amounts of nitrogen (N), phosphorus (P), and potassium (K) they contain. These elements are the major plant nutrients.

If you're interested in testing soil for nitrogen, phosphorus, and potassium, you may be able to obtain a test kit for them from a garden center or science supply company. *Caution: Follow the kit's directions carefully since chemical reagents supplied in the kit may be harmful. Keep chemical products locked up and out of reach of children.*

Chapter Ten

Making Mud

Here's the housekeeper's definition of soil: Dirt. Mud. Stuff from outside that enters the house by clinging to shoes, boots, and sometimes clothing. Sometimes odorous, it makes the house dirty.

Here are two textbook definitions of soil:

1. Soil is made up of loosely consolidated organic and inorganic material generally found on or near the surface of the earth.

2. Soil is earth material that has been so modified and acted upon by physical, chemical, and biological agents that it will support rooted plants.

Now it's your turn to be the physical, chemical, and biological agents and make your own soil. Then you can see if it will support plant life. Therefore, you'll want to aim for the perfect gardening soil.

- As a biological agent, you will collect dead plants and insects to compose the necessary 5 percent humus content of garden soil.

- As physical and chemical agents, you will break up rocks to compose the 45 percent mineral content of good garden soil.

- As good physical and chemical agents, you'll be sure to break the rocks into small pieces (less than 2 millimeters diameter) so that 25 percent air space will be present in the soil.

- The 25 percent water content of good garden soil will come from the tap.

•••••••••••••••••••••••••••••••••••••••

PROJECT

Compressing Years into Minutes: Quick Soil Making

Caution: To prevent possible injury from flying rock fragments, be sure to wear safety glasses, gloves, and long-sleeved clothing when breaking up rocks.

Note: Use sedimentary rocks if possible. Sedimentary rock (like sandstone and shale) breaks into small pieces with less effort than does igneous or metamorphic rock.

MATERIALS:

- Safety glasses
- Long-sleeved clothing (long pants, too)
- Gloves
- Hammer
- Newspaper, rags, or towels
- Small sedimentary rocks and pebbles
- Parts of dead plants and dead insects
- Pail or other container
- Old spoon for mixing
- Flowerpot or other potting container
- Quick-germinating seeds, such as bean or radish seeds
- Water

PROCEDURE:

1. Collect some small sedimentary rocks and pebbles. Remember that they will make up about 45 percent of your soil, so gather enough.
2. Collect some dead organic material—leaves, bark bits, and insects. You don't need a lot; this will only be about 5 percent of the soil you make.
3. Wrap the rocks and/or pebbles in several layers of newspaper, rags, or towels so that they are completely covered.
4. Wear safety glasses, gloves, and long-sleeved clothing, and work on a hard, indestructible surface (not your dining room table, but maybe on a workbench or in the driveway). Use the hammer to pound the wrapped rocks and/or pebbles until they break apart into small pieces less than 2 millimeters in diameter. Be patient—this may take time and muscle.

5. Place the ground-up rock into a pail or other container, removing any large pieces.

6. Shred the organic matter into very small fragments. You can probably do this with your gloved hands.

7. Place the organic fragments into the container with the crushed rock.

8. With the spoon, mix the materials in the container well. You now have dry soil. (Of course, in nature the process takes much longer—years and even centuries.)

9. Fill the flowerpot with the soil you mixed in step 8.

10. Plant a few seeds in the soil in the pot. Read the seed package for directions on how deep to plant the seeds.

11. Moisten the soil and seeds with water, preferably from the bottom of the pot so the soil does not become waterlogged.

12. Wait several days and watch for sprouts to appear. If you planted the seeds indoors, move the container to a sunny windowsill to encourage plant growth.

● ●

Activity

Using potting soil in another pot, plant the same type of seeds at the same time you plant the seeds in your homemade soil. Compare germination and growth of the seeds in the two soils.

Regional Soils

The soil you made will differ from what someone else makes in another part of the country or the world because rocks differ from one place to another. Soils that form naturally in different regions have different characteristics, too. These properties depend not only upon the soil's parent material but also upon the climate—humidity, precipitation, temperature—and the amount and kind of vegetation in the area. A soil map or earth science book will tell you the classification names of soils throughout the world.

On the North American continent, soils are one of two general types with many subtypes. In the eastern region where rainfall exceeds 65 centimeters (25.6 inches) per year, the soils are called *pedalfers* (*ped* for soil, *al* for aluminum, and *fer* for iron). These soils are generally rich in clay, iron oxides, and quartz fragments. They are poor in soluble minerals since those minerals are dissolved and leached out by the amount of precipitation.

Except for the Pacific coastal region, rainfall in the western part of North America is less than 65 centimeters (25.6 inches) per year. Here the soils are called *pedocals* (*pedo* for soil and *cal* for calcium). These soils are lower in clay and rich in calcium carbonate, which does not leach out because precipitation is less.

Volcanic Soil

Some of the richest soils on earth are volcanic soils. No, they don't spew out of active volcanoes, but form over time from volcanic rock that once flowed from a volcano. Volcanic soil is rich in minerals such as iron, aluminum, calcium, magnesium, sodium, titanium, potassium, manganese, and phosphates.

Volcanic soil is, logically, found in the neighborhood of volcanoes. Places like the Pacific Northwest and the Hawaiian Islands possess generous amounts of volcanic soil.

■■■

On the island of Hawaii, the black sand beaches are composed of volcanic rock that has been broken up by the ocean's action.

■■■

● ●

PROJECT

Make Volcanic Soil—Anywhere

If you don't live in an area where you can find volcanic rocks lying around, you can probably purchase some from a landscaping center or rock store. Nurseries and landscaping centers often sell scoria or pumice (types of volcanic rocks) as decorative rocks. They are lightweight, very porous (various-sized holes left by gases in the molten rock are visible), and may be red or gray in color.

Caution: To prevent possible injury from flying rock fragments, be sure to wear safety glasses, gloves, and long-sleeved clothing when breaking up rocks.

MATERIALS:

- Volcanic rock
- Safety glasses

- Long-sleeved clothing (long pants, too)
- Gloves
- Hammer
- Newspaper, rags, or towels
- Pail or other container
- Flowerpot or other potting container
- Quick-germinating seeds, such as bean or radish seeds
- Water

PROCEDURE:

1. Wrap the volcanic rocks in several layers of newspaper, rags, or towels so that they are completely covered.
2. Wear safety glasses, gloves, and long-sleeved clothing, and work on a hard, indestructible surface (not your dining room table, but maybe on a workbench or in the driveway). Use the hammer to pound the wrapped rocks until they break apart into small pieces less than 2 millimeters in diameter. Be patient—this may take time and muscle.
3. Place the ground-up rock into a pail or other container, removing any large pieces.
4. Fill the flowerpot with the ground-up volcanic rock.
5. Plant a few seeds in the pot. Read the seed package for directions on how deep to plant the seeds.
6. Moisten the soil and seeds with water, preferably from the bottom of the pot so the soil does not become waterlogged.
7. Wait several days and watch for sprouts to appear. If you planted the seeds indoors, move the container to a sunny windowsill to encourage plant growth.

● ●

Activity
You may want to make both volcanic soil and garden soil and plant seeds in them at the same time. Plant similar seeds in potting soil, too. Compare the plants' growth in all three kinds of soil.

Moon Soil

NASA (National Aeronautics and Space Administration) made soil from crushed moon rocks and found that plants grew well in it. Of course, plants wouldn't grow on the moon, since they also need water and air.

For Further Investigation:

• Use a 10X hand lens to examine the soil you made and compare it with what you see when you look at a soil sample you've gathered.

• Check the pH of your homemade garden and volcanic soil according to the directions in Chapter 9. How did pH affect the sprouting and growth of the seeds you planted in your homemade soil?

Chapter Eleven

Disappearing Dirt
....

The State of the World's Soil Resource

Since World War II, more than 3 billion acres of agricultural land have been damaged by human actions. That's an area larger than China and India combined. It's happened in less than fifty years and hasn't stopped. Restoration is complicated and extremely expensive.

Deforestation, cultivation, overgrazing, compaction of the soil by heavy machinery, construction of roads and buildings, and paving of parking lots are just some of the human activities that impact our soil resource.

Topsoil is still being lost at a greater rate than it can be replaced by lengthy, natural soil-building processes. What you did on a small scale with a hammer, rocks, and organic materials to make soil in a matter of minutes takes many years in nature.

Erosion, the wearing away of the earth's surface by the action of water, wind, or glacial ice, is a natural process. Its speed depends upon the resistance of the rock or soil that's being worn away. You can see what erosion does along streams and riverbanks and along lakes and seashores. Where the banks are so steep that vegetation cannot gain a foothold, water is free to erode the soil and rock layers. Layers of softer rock or rock that is not strongly cemented together are eroded more deeply, often undercutting harder, more resistant rock that remains as overhangs.

Human activity, however, can speed up erosion. For instance, plant roots help hold soil in place. But when all trees are removed from a piece of land and the soil is cultivated (which removes grasses and other natural plant cover), water running over the ground can easily wash away the top layer of soil. You can also see erosion at work at construction sites, where heavy downpours make gullies in exposed piles of soil.

Where does the eroded material go? Carried away by water and sometimes contaminated with fertilizers and other chemicals, it eventually finds its way to rivers, lakes, and the sea, where it is deposited on the bottom as sediment.

Wind can also blow exposed topsoil away. During the 1930s "Dust Bowl," wind eroded the dried-out cultivated land of the United States' Great Plains.

Although various human activities speed erosion, humans can also help slow erosion through projects like planting trees and shrubs on empty sloping land. The roots will both slow runoff water and hold the soil to prevent it from washing or blowing away.

Activity

Make two small piles of sand, one dry and one moist (outdoors or in a large, flat container, please). Blow across the tops of both piles with either your lung power or a hand-held hair dryer. What happens to the sand piles? You have just demonstrated erosion by wind.

Activity

Make a pile of small stones and soil (in a place where mud won't matter). Pour water over the pile and watch what happens. What's washed away? Where does it go? What's left behind? You have just demonstrated erosion by water.

Agricultural economist Lester R. Brown, president of the Worldwatch Institute in Washington, D.C., stated, "Each year the world's farmers are trying to feed 92 million more people with 24 billion tons less topsoil. . . . You don't have to have a Ph.D. in agronomy to understand that those two trends can't both continue indefinitely." In the United States alone, 25 percent of croplands are eroding faster than they can be preserved, according to estimates by the U.S. Soil Conservation Service.

The United Nations sponsored a 1992 survey to chart soil health around the world. Results indicate that

- nearly 22 million acres of the world's land can no longer support vegetation.
- to become productive, another 740 million acres will require a restoration effort greater than most developing nations could organize.
- an additional 2.3 billion acres—about the size of the entire United States land area—require major and costly reclamation efforts such as installation of drainage ditches.

James G. Speth, president of the World Resource Institute (WRI) in Washington, D.C., said that the United Nations soil survey "confirms our worst fears about the degree to which soils are eroding and being degraded around the planet. . . . If topsoil erosion continues at post–World War II rates, feeding an exploding world population could prove extremely difficult."

In addition to erosion from wind and water, the U.N. survey mapped soil degradation from chemical sources, such as excessive levels of salts or pollutants, and from physical sources such as livestock or heavy machinery. The U.N. team of roughly two hundred analysts reported that

- 35 percent of soil erosion results from livestock overgrazing. Not only can animals strip away plant cover, leaving topsoils bare and targets for erosion, but their trampling can also compact soil, reducing its ability to hold moisture.
- 30 percent of soil damage results from deforestation.
- 28 percent of soil degradation results from harmful agricultural practices, such as overfertilization or ignoring fallow periods.
- in North America, poor agricultural practices are the prominent cause of soil damage.

According to Allen L. Hammond, WRI's program director, parts of Africa, Asia, and South America have been especially hard hit by soil degradation—a problem that may be tied to poverty.

Here's a challenge: *Do something in your neighborhood that will improve soil health or prevent it from being eroded.*

Chapter 12

Minerals

• •

Pick up a rock—any rock. Hold it in your hand. Feel its texture. Look at it closely. Use a 10X hand lens to magnify it. Can you see similarly shaped, sized, and colored bits throughout?

Rocks are composed of minerals. You can see individual mineral particles in many rocks if you examine them closely. Because rocks and minerals go together, many people treat them as the same. But they're not. Think of a brick wall representing a rock. Minerals are like the individual bricks that make up the wall. There can be several different kinds in that wall just as there may be several different minerals in a rock.

There are thousands of minerals, but they all meet five requirements.

1. Minerals are inorganic. That means that minerals do not come from either plant or animal matter.
2. Minerals are formed in nature. Synthetic (man-made) substances, no matter how perfect, are not classified as minerals because they were not formed in nature. (However, there are some very good synthetic gems.)
3. Minerals are solid. They have a definite shape and a definite volume.
4. Minerals have definite internal atomic patterns. The atoms of a mineral are arranged in fixed positions specific to that mineral. This arrangement of atoms gives the mineral a geometric pattern. Each mineral will fall into one of six possible crystal families, or systems, which may be further divided into specific crystal forms:

- *Cubic* system, such as the minerals halite or galena
- *Tetragonal* system, such as zircon or rutile
- *Hexagonal* system, such as quartz or calcite
- *Orthorhombic* system, such as sulfur or topaz
- *Monoclinic* system, such as muscovite or augite
- *Triclinic* system, such as plagioclase feldspar or rhodonite

If you can see the pattern with the naked eye, the mineral specimen is called a crystal. If the crystal pattern is so small that its tiny crystals are visible only under a microscope, it is called massive.

5. Minerals have exact chemical compositions. That means a mineral is always composed of the same kind of atoms. For example, all quartz anywhere in the world is made up of oxygen and silicon atoms. (By the way, oxygen and silicon are the two most abundant elements in the lithosphere.) Most minerals are composed of one or more of these eight elements: oxygen, silicon, aluminum, iron, calcium, sodium, potassium, and magnesium.

What do minerals mean to you? Do you like jewelry? Gems are minerals. Do you want to find a fortune? Try panning for gold. (You may not have to go too far. Our home state of Ohio seems an unlikely place to find gold, but in the southern part of the state, panning sometimes yields gold.) Do you like to collect things? Finding and collecting minerals can be great fun, and excellent specimens may be worth large sums of money. Would you like to discuss minerals with other interested people? There are mineralogy clubs scattered across North America, often connected with natural history or geology museums. To find one near you, see the list of museums in the Appendix.

GEMS, MINERALS, AND JEWELRY:

Some people say, "I like gems, but I don't care about minerals." How are minerals and gems related? Are they the same? Different?

- Naturally occurring gems are minerals, but not all minerals are gems.
- Gems are rare minerals that are beautiful and durable.
- There are two divisions of gems.

  1. *Precious stones,* such as diamonds and emeralds, are the rarest and therefore most valuable.
  2. *Semi-precious stones,* such as jade, amethysts, garnets, turquoise, and opals, are more common and hence not as valuable as precious stones.

These two divisions are not absolute and vary with different cultures and throughout history.

• Synthetic gems, though lovely, are not minerals.

Gems are often set into jewelry, which is usually crafted of precious metals. The designation of gems and metals as "precious" has changed over time. Before Charles Hall invented an inexpensive way to refine aluminum in 1886, aluminum was extremely expensive to produce and therefore rare and precious. In 1886, worldwide aluminum production was less than 100 pounds (220.5 kilograms), and aluminum cost more than $5.00 per pound—a great sum of money at that time. Kings and queens around the world had their crowns made of aluminum.

That's changed now. Aluminum is inexpensive and common. What would your friends say if you wore aluminum jewelry? What would you think of a monarch with an aluminum crown today?

■■■

It's pretty easy to look at a ring and recognize the stone as turquoise or at earrings and recognize opal. But what about minerals that can't be identified that easily? Sometimes it requires investigative mineralogy to discover the identity of a mineral in question. Put on your detective hat or lab coat and imagine yourself the Sherlock Holmes, Robert Ballard, or Marie Curie of minerals. Get ready to perform some mineral investigations yourself.

Physical Properties of Minerals

Each mineral has characteristic physical properties. Some properties, because they're common to several minerals, only *help* in identification. Others are dead giveaways because they are unique to individual minerals. Most often, though, the different physical characteristics of a mineral specimen must be considered together to reveal the mineral's identity. It's as if each mineral has its own fingerprint.

Physical properties of minerals are:

• Color
• Luster
• Streak
• Hardness
• Magnetism
• Specific Gravity
• Cleavage
• Fracture

You may want to visit your local library or bookstore to obtain information on rock and mineral identification. Worthwhile books will list specific physical properties for each mineral included.

Color

Color can help identify a mineral, but very few minerals can be identified by color alone. In fact, many minerals present themselves in a variety of different colors. Topaz, for instance—the November birthstone—can be colorless (clear), yellow, green, blue, or red. The most popular color of topaz for gemstones has been a rich orange-yellow. Quartz is another example of a mineral that has several different colors: clear, white, pink, and purple. Even diamonds aren't all the same color. Although most are colorless, they may also be yellow, brown, green, blue, or red. On the other hand, two minerals that possess only one color are sulfur (bright yellow) and cinnabar (red).

Most minerals contain traces of impurities that can affect their color. In some instances, impurities make a mineral more valuable. Quartz, as mentioned above, may be purple. The color results from an impurity—a trace of manganese. Purple quartz is the semiprecious gemstone known as amethyst. Besides color variation caused by impurities, some minerals change color or tarnish quickly when exposed to air and precipitation.

Luster

Luster (or *lustre*) is the absorption, reflection, or refraction of light by a mineral's surface. Disregarding color, what does the mineral's surface look like?

Two basic divisions of luster are *metallic* and *nonmetallic*. Metallic mineral surfaces look like metal—shiny and reflective. Galena is one example of a mineral with metallic luster.

Nonmetallic mineral surfaces do not look like metal. Dolomite is an example of a common nonmetallic mineral. Here's where luster becomes fun. A number of other self-explanatory terms help to further describe nonmetallic luster: glassy, dull, earthy, silky, greasy, pearly, and resinous. These aren't absolute terms, but you can use them to give an idea of a mineral's appearance. Maybe you can come up with a better word to describe some of these lusters.

- *Metallic* minerals shine like the polished surface of a metal.
- *Vitreous* minerals look like glass.
- *Resinous* minerals have the luster of resin.
- *Greasy* minerals look as if they were covered with a thin layer of oil.
- *Adamantine* minerals have a hard, brilliant luster.

- *Pearly* minerals look like pearls.
- *Earthy* minerals have the powdery, crumbly look of compacted soil.
- *Silky* minerals have a fibrous sheen like that of rayon or silk.
- *Dull* minerals have surfaces showing little reflectivity.

Streak

Streak is another mineral property related to color. It is the color of the mineral's powder. Unlike the color of the mineral itself, which may vary among samples of the same mineral, streak is nearly always the same for any sample of that mineral. For instance, topaz may be different colors, but its streak is always colorless. Dolomite's color may be white, pink, gray, green, or black, but it always has a white streak.

To see streak, you need a piece of unglazed white porcelain or ceramic tile, referred to as a "streak plate," and a mineral sample. When a mineral is rubbed across the streak plate, the color of the mark left there is the mineral's streak. A potential problem with using a streak plate occurs when the mineral sample is harder than the streak plate itself. If this is the case, the mineral won't leave any powder behind but will cut into the streak plate.

Hardness

Mineral hardness is expressed as a number from 1 (softest) through 10 (hardest) on the Mohs scale of hardness (named after the German mineralogist Friedrich Mohs). Ten index minerals of known hardness are the basis of this scale.

1. Talc (used to make talcum powder)
2. Gypsum
3. Calcite
4. Fluorite
5. Apatite
6. Orthoclase
7. Quartz
8. Topaz
9. Corundum
10. Diamond

The Mohs scale is used in this way: If a mineral of unknown hardness scratches a certain mineral of known hardness, the unknown is harder than the known. If the mineral of unknown hardness won't scratch a particular mineral of known hardness, the unknown is softer than the known.

Of course, most people don't have a set of Mohs scale index minerals in their closets. In that case, several common items can determine hardness range:

- Your fingernail has a hardness of 2.5.
- A copper penny has a hardness of 3 (the same as calcite).
- A knife blade or window glass has a hardness of 5.5.
- A steel file has a hardness of 6.5.

So if an unknown mineral scratches a penny, it is harder than 3. But if it won't scratch glass it is softer than 5.5. The unknown mineral therefore has a hardness range of 3 to 5.5.

Many people think that only diamonds scratch glass. The truth is, many different minerals will scratch glass.

Magnetism

Magnetism is helpful in identifying a few minerals. Only a couple of minerals are naturally magnetic: magnetite (or lodestone) and pyrrhotite. A few others like manganese, nickel, and iron-titanium ores may become magnetic when heated.

Caution: Do not heat minerals. They may explode and the fragments could cause injury. It is not necessary to heat minerals (or rocks) in order to identify them.

Specific Gravity

One of the best ways to identify a mineral is to calculate its *specific gravity*. Specific gravity is the ratio of the mass of an object (in this case, a mineral) to the mass of an equal volume of water. (Unfortunately for mineral detectives, the specific gravity of some minerals can vary as much as 25 percent from sample to sample.) After you measure specific gravity a few times, you'll notice that the greater the specific gravity (the larger the number), the heavier the specimen will feel.

Halite (salt) has a specific gravity of 2.1. Galena (lead ore) has a specific gravity of 7.5. Gold's specific gravity is 19.3.

GLIMMERING GOLD

With a specific gravity of 19.3, gold is so heavy compared to most other minerals that it is hard to fool someone who knows minerals.

Gold is beautiful. It's shiny and reflective. It's . . . well, it's . . . gold! But not only its beauty makes it widely used in jewelry. It is desirable for jewelry making because it's so easy to work with—it's malleable. On the Mohs scale, gold checks in at a mere 2.5, a soft metal.

But because gold is so heavy, you can pan for it in rivers and streams. Water washes away the lighter rock and leaves the heavier gold behind.

Gold seekers are sometimes fooled by pyrite, called "fool's gold." Those in the know about minerals, however, won't be fooled. Pyrite has a hardness of 6.5, a specific gravity of about 5, and a greenish black streak.

■■

Cleavage

Cleavage is the way some minerals split along planes. Cleavage determines the shape of mineral crystals and is responsible for the lovely crystals often displayed in museums. But in the field, cleavage may be difficult to determine. And some minerals do not cleave—that is, they do not split in characteristic patterns.

A couple of the best examples of common minerals with clearly observable cleavage are mica and clear calcite (also called Iceland spar). Mica has *basal* cleavage. That means you can peel off layers like sheets of paper. Clear calcite has *rhombohedral* cleavage. Crystals with this cleavage have the optical property of bending light two ways so you'll see double if you look through it.

Fracture

Minerals that have *fracture* do not reveal their crystal patterns when split. They simply break into pieces of random size and shape. Many minerals fall into this category, so it is certainly not a reliable test on which to base identification.

Minerals can be identified, however, by determining as many of their properties as accurately as possible. Once you discover a sample's "fingerprint," it's easy to identify it.

●●●●●●●●●●●●●●●●●●●●●●●●●●●●●●●●●●●●●●

PROJECT

Cataloging Mineral Samples

If you can find mineral samples in your area, collect some. They will be rocks that seem the same throughout—the same color, same texture, same surface appearance. If you can't find any rocks that look like they might be minerals, you can obtain mineral sets (no fair peeking at the names) from science and hobby supply stores. See the "Science Supplies" section of the Appendix for companies that offer mineral sets by mail.

MATERIALS:

- Mineral samples
- Quick-drying, light-colored enamel
- Small paintbrush
- Fine-point permanent marker
- Index cards or paper
- Pen or pencil

PROCEDURE:

1. Place a small spot of quick-drying enamel on each specimen.
2. Label each specimen with a number. Use a permanent marker to write a number on the spot of enamel on each mineral sample.
3. On an index card (use one card for each sample) or sheet of paper, record the following:
   - Specimen number
   - Location where specimen was found
   - Collector's name (You!)
   - Date found
   - Name of mineral, if known, or add name later when you identify it.

In this way, you can catalog all your minerals, as well as rocks.

PROJECT

Color, Luster, Streak

MATERIALS:

- Mineral samples
- Paper and pen(cil)
- Streak plate (a piece of unglazed white tile) *Hint*: You can use the unglazed back side of common floor or wall tiles.

PROCEDURE:

1. Make four columns on a sheet of paper. Label them as follows:

   - Number of specimen/Name
   - Color
   - Luster
   - Streak

2. In the first column, list the numbers that you assigned to your samples and their names, if known.
3. In the second column, list the color of each specimen.
4. In the third column, note the luster of each specimen. First, determine whether it's metallic (it looks like metal) or nonmetallic (it does not look like metal). If it's nonmetallic, decide whether it's glassy, dull, earthy, silky, greasy, pearly, or resinous.
5. Drag each specimen quickly across the streak plate and record the color of the powder streak in the fourth column. Check that the mineral specimen does not scratch the streak plate. (If it does, it is harder than the streak plate and may not leave a powder streak.)

As you work with different mineral samples, do you find a pattern of color, luster, and streak?

PROJECT

Hardness

If you don't have a set of index minerals for hardness comparison, you can use several common items. You may want to make another column on your worksheet from the previous project to record your samples' hardnesses.

MATERIALS:

- Mineral specimens
- Copper penny
- Knife blade or window glass. *Caution: Be careful when using a knife or piece of glass with sharp edges. Make sure you get permission from an adult to use it. You should wear gloves and tape all but one corner of the edges of the glass with masking tape.*
- Steel file

PROCEDURE:

1. For each mineral specimen, check whether you can scratch it with your fingernail. If your fingernail scratches it, the mineral has a hardness of less than (<) 2.5. If not, the hardness is greater than (>) 2.5.

2. See whether a penny will scratch each mineral specimen's surface. If the penny scratches it, the mineral's hardness is less than (<) 3. If not, the hardness is greater than (>) 3.

3. For each mineral specimen, check whether a knife blade or piece of window glass scratches it. If so, the mineral's hardness is less than (<) 5.5. If the opposite happens and it scratches the glass, the hardness is greater than (>) 5.5.

4. For each mineral specimen, check whether a steel file will scratch it. If so, the mineral's hardness is less than (<) 6.5. If not, the hardness is greater than (>) 6.5.

5. Record a hardness range for each of your mineral specimens, for example: greater than (>) 3 but less than (<) 5.5.

● ●

When you've determined color, luster, streak, and hardness, you've narrowed the search for an unknown mineral's identity. You may be able to identify it on just these points by comparing your results to a listing of known mineral properties that you can find in reference books.

Activity
Check the magnetism of your mineral samples using a pocket compass. If the compass needle follows a mineral as you move it around the compass, the mineral is magnetic. Should a sample be magnetic, you can be sure it is one of these minerals: magnetite (lodestone) or pyrrhotite.

● ●

PROJECT
Specific Gravity

Specific gravity can be extremely helpful in mineral identification. You can make another column on your worksheet chart to record specific gravity for each mineral specimen.

MATERIALS:

- Mineral sample(s)
- Spring scale
- String
- Glass or beaker
- Water
- Paper and pen(cil)

PROCEDURE:

1. Weigh the mineral specimen in the air. Tie the specimen on a piece of string, then tie the other end of the string to the hook on the end of a spring scale and record the mineral's weight. This weight will be *A*.

Figure 12-1. Weighing a mineral sample in air.

Figure 12-2. Weighing a mineral specimen in water.

2. Fill the glass or beaker about three-quarters full with water.
3. Keep the mineral hanging from the scale as in step 1, but this time let the specimen hang into the water so the rock is completely covered with water and not touching the sides or bottom of the glass or beaker. Record the rock's weight in this position. This weight will be *B*. *Hint*: The weight should be less than it was in air.
4. Subtract the mineral's weight in water (*B*) from its weight in air (*A*) and record the answer (*C*): $A - B = C$.
5. Divide *A* (dry weight) by *C* (determined in step 4). The answer is the specimen's specific gravity: $A \div C = $ Specific gravity.

Activity

Although you probably have enough information to identify your mineral samples by now, examine them for cleavage or fracture and record your findings on your worksheet chart.

- If you can see consistent crystals in your specimen, it has cleavage. You may want to use a 10X hand lens. If the crystals are large enough and accessible, you can place the specimen on a clean sheet of paper and trace the crystals' sides and angles. Then you can measure the angles with a protractor. Using a reference book, you may be able to name the specific crystal form.
- If you can't see consistent crystal shapes in your mineral specimen, it has fracture. Note that on your worksheet.

Note: It is not necessary to split your samples with a hammer to see how they break apart. (You may end up with a bunch of little pieces that aren't worth keeping.) If you have an extremely large sample and want to break it apart, wrap it in an old towel or cloth first to prevent flying fragments. Be sure to wear goggles or safety glasses, gloves, and long-sleeved clothing.

Using your worksheet chart and any crystal sketches you may have drawn, you can put the pieces together and solve the puzzle to confirm the identities of your mineral samples. Who knows what will turn up?

You'll want to visit a library to consult reference books on minerals. Perhaps the geology department of a nearby college or university has reference materials to help you. A local university or museum may have a mineral collection that you can view. To find one near you, see the list of museums in the Appendix. In Canada, the Geological Survey of Canada offers free posters on minerals and gemstones. See the resources listed in the Appendix for more information.

Further information may be available from mining companies or manufacturing firms that use minerals as raw materials. Maybe you can connect with a geologist or mineralogist who works for one of these companies and discuss your common interest in minerals, as well as learn more about careers in the field. A geological, gemological, or mineralogical society may meet in your neighborhood (or you can start one)—this is a great way to meet people who share your interest.

Table 12-1. CHARACTERISTICS OF SOME COMMON MINERALS

Name	Color	Streak	Hardness	Specific Gravity	Shape
Apatite	White, Yellow, Brown, Blue, Green	White	5	3.2	Hexagonal Massive
Augite	Black to Dark Green	Colorless	6	3.5	Monoclinic
Calcite	White, Varied	White	3	2.7	Hexagonal Massive
Copper	Copper Red	Copper Red	3	8.1	Cubic
Corundum	Brown, Green, Pink, Blue, Red, Black, Violet	Colorless	9	3.9–4.1	Hexagonal Massive
Dolomite	White to Pink, Gray, Green, Black	White	3.5–4	2.8	Hexagonal
Feldspar orthoclase	White, Gray, Red, Green (rare)	Colorless	6	2.5	Monoclinic Massive
Feldspar plagioclase	Gray, Green, White	Colorless	6	2.5	Monoclinic Massive
Fluorite	White, Green, Yellow, Purple, Red, Blue	Colorless	4	3–3.3	Cubic Octahedral
Galena	Gray	Gray	2.5	7.5	Cubic
Garnet	Yellow, Red	Colorless	7.5	3.5	Cubic

Mineral	Color	Streak	Hardness	Specific Gravity	Crystal System
Graphite	Black, Gray	Black	1–2	2.3	Hexagonal
Halite	Colorless, Reddish, White, Blue	Colorless	2.5	2.1	Cubic
Hematite	Reddish Brown to Black	Reddish Brown	6	5.3	Hexagonal Massive
Hornblende	Green to Black	Gray to White	5–6	3.4	Monoclinic
Limonite	Yellow, Brown, Black	Yellowish Brown	5.5	4.0	Massive
Magnetite	Black	Black	6	5.2	Cubic
Mica Biotite	Black to Brown	Colorless	2.5	2.8–3.4	Monoclinic
Mica Muscovite	White to Light Gray	Colorless	2.5	2.8	Monoclinic
Olivine	Olive Green	Colorless	6.5	3.5	Orthorhombic
Pyrite	Light, Brassy Yellow	Greenish Black	6.5	5.0	Cubic
Quartz	Colorless to Various Colors	Colorless	7	2.65	Hexagonal
Sulfur	Yellow	Yellow to White	2.5	2.0	Orthorhombic
Talc	White, Greenish	White	1	2.8	Monoclinic Massive
Topaz	Colorless, White, Yellow, Pale Blue, Pink, Red, Green	Colorless	8	3.5–3.6	Orthorhombic

Chapter Thirteen

Bits of the Earth's Crust
••

Rocks

When you were a child, you probably enjoyed picking up stones at the beach or along a creek bank and throwing them into the water. You liked the splashes they made. You discovered that larger stones made larger splashes. You liked the "plop-plop" sounds of little ones hitting the water. The large ones that were almost too heavy for you to lift made wonderful "galoonk" sounds. Maybe you even learned to skip stones across the water's surface. You found that flat, light ones worked best. You may have put some into your pockets to bring home.

At first you may not have looked at the rocks you picked up, but then you noticed that they were different colors. Some were prettier than others. Maybe you saved the pretty ones you gathered and threw the not-so-pretty ones into the water. Perhaps the pretty ones made it into a bag or box as your rock collection. You may even have sorted them by color or size.

Now get that box or bag out of the back corner of your closet and take another look at the rocks inside. Or pick up a few stones—from your yard, the beach, or a gravel parking lot. Examine them closely, even with a magnifying glass or 10X hand lens. What do you see? Do you see specks of similar material? Or are there individual large particles of material that look quite different? Feel their surfaces. Are they smooth or rough and grainy? Are some heavier than others?

Every stone is a piece of the earth and has a story to tell. Loose rocks and stones come from the bedrock of the earth's crust. It's below land and sea. In some places bedrock forms outcrops. Where it doesn't, it can be found below the soil.

Rocks are naturally formed aggregates (combinations) of minerals. The minerals discussed in Chapter 12 are combined and cemented together in various combinations to produce the variety of rocks that populate the earth's crust. Some are colorful; some are blah. Some are soft; some are hard. Some contain fossils; others don't. Some were formed from once-living (organic) material; others began as molten material deep in the earth.

Classifying Rocks

Different rock types are common in different areas of the world. According to their origins, your specimens can be classified as igneous, sedimentary, or metamorphic. The samples of surface rocks you've gathered may all be of the same classification, or you may have samples from two or even all three categories.

Igneous Rock

Igneous rock forms when molten material (*magma*) cools and solidifies. Igneous rocks have a crystalline appearance with the crystals mixed throughout, not in layers. Igneous rock can be further categorized into two types: plutonic and volcanic.

If magma cools and crystallizes deep within the earth, *plutonic,* or *intrusive,* rocks result. Because they form beneath other earth layers, the magma cools very slowly. Plutonic rocks are usually coarse grained and contain crystals large enough to be identified with the naked eye.

Magma that reaches the earth's surface flows as lava or explodes to form ash. *Volcanic,* or *extrusive,* rocks form when magma fills cracks in the earth at the surface or is deposited on the earth's surface by a volcano. Volcanic rocks are finer grained than plutonic rocks and some, like obsidian, are even glassy.

Basalt, usually dull black or gray and volcanic, is the most common kind of igneous rock on earth or in the earth. Other common igneous rocks are granite and pumice. If you can't find any granite stones in your vicinity, look at the gravestones in a cemetery—many are fashioned of polished granite. Granite is plutonic and you can see its individual crystals of feldspar and quartz. Pumice is volcanic and is often used in landscaping because it's relatively lightweight.

Igneous rock is considered to be primary-origin rock as opposed to secondary-origin sedimentary rock. According to geologists, igneous rock is the oldest rock type on earth. Yet new igneous rocks are formed whenever there is volcanic activity.

Sedimentary Rock

Have you gathered any stones that seem like they may have broken away from other rock in layers? They are probably in the sedimentary classification.

Sedimentary rocks form at the earth's surface by the accumulation of sediment (solid material in suspension) in water (*aqueous* deposits) or from air (*eolian* deposits). The sediment may be pieces of minerals and fragments of other rock, organic particles (the remains of animals or plants), products of evaporation and other chemical processes, or a combination of two or more of these. Because they are deposited in nearly flat layers, or beds, sedimentary rocks have a layered appearance. They are relatively soft, usually break easily, and often feel gritty.

Sedimentary rocks fall into two categories. *Clastic* sedimentary rocks are composed of fragments of pre-existing rocks. *Nonclastic* sedimentary rocks are those that formed by chemical and organic processes.

Because suspended particles tend to settle out of water or air by weight—heaviest first, lightest last—sedimentary rocks usually contain particles of similar size. An exception, *conglomerate,* consists of rock fragments and particles of various sizes from sand grains to pebbles.

Sandstone (you can tell what it's made of by its name) is a common sedimentary rock often used in building. Other common sedimentary rocks are *shale,* made up of extremely fine mud, clay, and silt particles; and *limestone,* often used in construction and as driveway stone.

Sedimentary rock is where fossils are found. Coal, a fossil fuel, is a sedimentary rock.

Metamorphic Rock

Existing rock can be altered by tremendous heat, pressure, or chemical action of contained fluids. Rock that has been altered in these ways is *metamorphic* rock. Although rock does not melt under the heat or pressure of metamorphism, its crystalline structure is changed and new minerals formed. Metamorphic rocks are very hard and more crystalline than igneous rocks. Often the crystals line up in bands.

When the different minerals in metamorphic rocks separate into parallel layers or parallel bands, the rocks are *foliated.* If parallel layers or bands are not present in metamorphic rocks, they are *nonfoliated.*

Metamorphism takes place deep within the earth's crust—too deep for direct observation—and over long periods of time. Geologists, therefore, do not fully understand the process. A few types of metamorphism have been duplicated in laboratory settings, with minerals such as quartz being converted to cristobalite above the temperature of 1470 degrees Celsius.

When sandstone undergoes metamorphism it becomes quartzite. Granite becomes gneiss (pronounced "nice"). Marble and slate are common metamorphic rocks. Marble is the metamorphic counterpart of limestone and is often used in buildings (as ornamental stonework) and as gravestones. Slate was once shale; it is used as roofing material and for the base of pool table playing surfaces. If you go to an old town or a residential neighborhood in an older section of a city, you may find sidewalks made of slate slabs. Slate was also used for chalkboards and individual writing slates. As the old song "School Days" says, "You wrote on my *slate*, 'I love you so.' "

Activity

• Look around for older homes that do not have brick, cement block, or other manufactured materials used for their foundations. What does the foundation rock look like (assuming it hasn't been painted over)? Very old homes may have foundations of random-sized rocks. These were probably stones found at the site or in nearby fields and fitted together. Some of them may be sandstone, but a variety of rock types may be present. If the foundations are of rectangular blocks of brown to yellowish to gray stone with a sandy appearance, they're probably sandstone. The blocks were most likely cut at a nearby quarry.

• Look for older city or town buildings and churches whose exteriors may be sandstone or limestone. Often the stone has darkened or even turned black because of weathering and air pollution. Many nineteenth-century stone structures in northeast Ohio, for example, are made of Berea Sandstone, named for one of the towns where this rock layer was quarried. In the early twentieth century, Salem or Indiana Limestone was brought to the Cleveland area from quarries in south-central Indiana and used in building construction. You may even find fossils in the limestone used on building exteriors. Some buildings may have pillars or columns, cornerstones, or insets that differ from the main types of stone used for the rest of the structure.

■■■■■■■■■■■■■■■■■■■■■■■■■■■■■■■■

GEODES

Have you seen a geode? Do you have one? They are often displayed in rock shops, by collectors, and in museums.

Geodes are spherical lumps of stone usually found in limestone. The outer rim is a kind of silica called chalcedony. When geodes are split open they look like miniature caverns lined with crystals of quartz or calcite extending inward from the hard outer rim.

Occasionally a geode collector gets lucky. One kid bought an unopened geode for a few dollars. When he cracked it open, there was gold inside. His find caused quite a stir.

Although sedimentary in origin (limestone), geodes can be classification puzzlers because of the large visible crystals inside. Geodes are believed to have been formed by mineral-laden waters. The water probably dissolved the limestone to form the hollows. Later the crystals were deposited inside them.

■■

Identifying Rocks

From the previous chapter, you already have experience identifying minerals. Since each kind of rock is composed of a specific combination of minerals, it makes sense that determining what minerals are present in a rock will enable you to put a name with the rock. This works well if you can see the individual minerals present in the rocks. But we can do this only with some kinds of igneous and metamorphic rocks. Individual minerals are simply not visible in many rocks.

So to help identify rocks in the following activities, we'll look at these characteristics:

• Color
• Texture (how the rock feels)
• Visible layers
• Other properties that can be identified, including the presence of specific minerals, the presence of fossils, and weight
• Classification as igneous, sedimentary, or metamorphic
• Response to acid

As you did when you identified minerals, you can record information about your rock samples on a worksheet chart. List the number or name (if known) of each specimen in the first column and label the other columns according to the criteria listed above. When the chart is completed, you can compare the characteristics of each specimen with lists of rock properties found in reference books or at the end of this chapter.

PROJECT

Cataloging Rocks

If you haven't collected a number of different rocks, do so now. You can also purchase rocks from rock shops, at museums, or through mail-order science supply catalogs.

MATERIALS:

- Rock samples
- Quick-drying, light-colored enamel
- Small paintbrush
- Fine-point permanent marker
- Index cards or paper
- Pen(cil)

PROCEDURE:

1. Place a small spot of quick-drying enamel on each specimen.
2. Label each specimen with a number. Use a permanent marker to write a number on the spot of enamel on each rock sample.
3. On an index card (use one card for each sample) or sheet of paper, record the following:
   - Specimen number
   - Location where specimen was found
   - Collector's name (You!)
   - Date found
   - Name of rock, if known, or add name later when you identify it.

Catalog all your rocks in this way.

PROJECT

The Hard Facts About Rocks

MATERIALS:

- Rock samples
- Worksheet chart

- Pen(cil)
- 10X hand lens or magnifying glass

PROCEDURE:

1. Place the number or name (it's more fun if you haven't looked up the name yet) of each rock specimen in the first column of your chart.
2. In the second column, record the specimen's color. If it's more than one color, record them all (pink and gray, for example). List the most abundant color first, the least abundant color last.
3. How does the rock specimen feel in your hand?
   - If it seems smooth and you can't see individual particles in it, record it as fine grained.

     Note: Beach stones that have been smoothed by constant water action over a long period of time will feel smooth. If you're working with beach stones, smoothness doesn't matter. Instead, pay special attention to the visibility of individual particles.
   - If it feels somewhat rough or sandy and you can see some individual particles, call it coarse grained.
   - If it is very rough and particles are easily visible, call it extremely coarse grained.

■■■■■■■■■■■■■■■■■■■■■■■■■■■■■■■■■■■■■■

GRAINS OF TRUTH

Grain alone does not determine whether a rock specimen is igneous, sedimentary, or metamorphic.

- Some volcanic igneous rocks are glassy in texture. Obsidian, in fact, is called "nature's glass."
- Other igneous rocks, like basalt, are fine grained.
- Some sedimentary rocks, like shale, are fine grained. Slate, a metamorphic rock, is also very smooth and fine grained.
- Granite is a coarse-grained igneous rock in which different minerals are visible, although it may appear fine grained if it has been weathered.
- Sandstone is a coarse-grained sedimentary rock in which the particles of sand are visible.
- Unweathered schist, a metamorphic rock, is coarse grained.
- Pumice, an igneous rock, has an abrasive feel to it because of all the cavities it contains. The rock itself is glassy, however.

• Conglomerate, an extremely coarse-grained sedimentary rock, can contain pebbles of $1/16$-inch in diameter to boulders more than 10 inches in diameter.

■■■

4. Does the rock specimen contain visible layers? Do they appear as layers that might be separated or are they more like bands of minerals? Describe the layers in the fourth column of your chart.
    • A number of sedimentary rocks have visible layers. The layers of shale may sometimes even be pulled apart.
    • In foliated metamorphic rocks, like gneiss, you can see banded layers containing different minerals.
    • Granite, an igneous rock, can occasionally give the appearance of having layers depending upon the arrangement of the minerals in it.
5. In the next column of your chart, record any other characteristics or properties you can observe or identify. Some of these might be:
    • Weight. If it's light, does it float in water? Pumice does because of all the cavities in it.
    • Appearances. Does it look like some other material? Obsidian looks like glass.
    • Minerals. Can you identify individual minerals in it? List them if you can.
    • Fossils. Limestone and sandstone may contain fossils. If the specimen has visible fossils, it's sedimentary.
    • Odor. Oil shale, for instance, may smell oily.
    These characteristics or properties do not necessarily have to be scientific, but they should be something you can identify or observe in the specimen.
6. In the second-to-last column of your chart, record the specimen's classification, if known. Make an educated guess if you don't know for sure.
    • If you can see individual minerals and they don't flow together, it's likely to be igneous.
    • If it has layers of similar particles, it's almost surely sedimentary.
    • If the minerals in it look stretched out or run together in a flow, it may be metamorphic.

PROJECT

The Acid Test

Rocks containing lime or calcite, which are alkaline, will fizz or *effervesce* when acid is applied to them. An acid test can safely be performed with strong vinegar. Vinegar, however, may not be a strong enough acid to react with rocks having low concentrations of calcite or lime.

Caution: When performing this experiment wear safety goggles, rubber gloves, and a lab coat or apron. Use an eyedropper to dispense the vinegar. After applying vinegar, rinse the rock, eyedropper, rubber gloves, and beaker or glass bowl thoroughly with water before handling them.

MATERIALS:

- Rock samples
- Goggles
- Rubber gloves
- Lab coat or apron
- Container such as a large beaker or glass bowl
- White vinegar (do not dilute)
- Eyedropper
- Worksheet chart

PROCEDURE:

1. To perform this experiment safely, wear goggles, rubber gloves, and a lab coat or apron.
2. Place a rock specimen in the beaker or glass bowl, and place the beaker or bowl in a sink or on several layers of newspaper.
3. Using the eyedropper, apply several drops of vinegar to the rock's surface.
4. Watch for signs of effervescing—bubbles and fizzing or a hissing sound.
5. In the final column of your worksheet chart, record whether or not the rock specimen effervesced. If it did, it's probably limestone.
6. Wash all equipment thoroughly.

• •

Now that you've gathered data on your rock specimens, you're ready to identify them. Don't get discouraged if you can't identify your samples right away. Detective work takes time.

You'll want to visit a library to consult reference books on rocks. Perhaps the geology department of a nearby college or university has reference materials to help you. A local university or museum might have a rock collection that you can view.

Further information may be available from companies that quarry stone. They may have geologists who can help you if you're stumped. A geological society may meet in your neighborhood (or you can start one)—it's a great way to meet people who share your interest.

The Geological Survey of Canada offers a free pamphlet and poster on rocks. For more information, see the resources listed at the end of the book.

Table 13-1. IGNEOUS ROCK

Name	Origin	Texture	Dominant Minerals
Obsidian	Extrusive	Glassy	Orthoclase feldspar, Amphibole, Quartz
Pumice	Extrusive	Fine grained	Orthoclase feldspar, Amphibole, Quartz
Scoria	Extrusive	Fine grained	Plagioclase feldspar, Olivine, Pyroxine
Rhyolite	Extrusive	Fine grained	Orthoclase feldspar, Amphibole, Quartz, Mica
Basalt	Extrusive	Fine grained	Plagioclase feldspar, Olivine, Pyroxine, Mica
Granite	Intrusive	Coarse grained	Orthoclase feldspar, Amphibole, Quartz, Mica
Diorite	Intrusive	Coarse grained	Plagioclase feldspar, Pyroxine, Amphibole, Mica
Gabbro	Intrusive	Coarse grained	Plagioclase feldspar, Pyroxine

Table 13-2. SEDIMENTARY ROCK

Name	Clastic/Nonclastic	Composition
Conglomerate	Clastic	Any kind of rock or mineral
Sandstone	Clastic	Quartz, or Feldspar and quartz
Siltstone	Clastic	Mostly quartz, some clay
Shale	Clastic	Mostly clay, some mica
Limestone	Nonclastic	Calcite or microscopic shells
Chert (Flint)	Nonclastic	Chalcedony
Alabaster	Nonclastic	Gypsum
Rock Salt	Nonclastic	Halite
Coal	Nonclastic	Fossilized plant material, carbon

Table 13-3. METAMORPHIC ROCK

Name	Layers	Origin
Slate	Foliated	Shale and Siltstone
Phyllite	Foliated	Shale and Siltstone
Schist	Foliated	Extrusive igneous rock, Shale, Siltstone, impure Limestone
Gneiss	Foliated	Intrusive igneous rock, Shale, Siltstone, impure Sandstone, Conglomerate
Marble	Nonfoliated	Pure limestone
Quartzite	Nonfoliated	Pure sandstone
Serpentine	Nonfoliated	Basalt

Chapter Fourteen

Relics from the Past

Fossils

What Is a Fossil?

No, fossil doesn't mean that old teacher you had last year. The word *fossil* refers to the remains or other evidence of plant and animal life before the beginning of recorded history. These remains have been preserved in the earth's crust by natural processes. In addition to plant and animal parts, fossils include footprints, tracks and trails, burrows of worms and rodents, eggs, gastroliths (stomach stones), and coprolites (fossilized excrement). The oldest known fossils are traces of microscopic algae and bacteria that paleontologists (scientists who study fossils) date at about 3 billion years old.

We recognize many fossils by their similarity in form to plants and animals that are now living, just as Aristotle recognized fossil shells because of their similarity to living sea creatures he observed. Aristotle noted in *Meteorics,* written about 330 B.C., that the fossil shells embedded in layers of rock near the seashore were like the shells of living sea creatures found in his day.

In the Middle Ages, and for several centuries thereafter, it was believed that fossils were either unfinished models of God's handiwork or else the remains of creatures deposited on the land by the Great Flood or Deluge described in the Book of Genesis in the Bible. Dr. John Woodward, a fossil collector of the seventeenth century, wrote in his essay *Toward a Natural*

History of the Earth (1695), "Marine bodies were borne forth of the sea by the Universal Deluge and upon the return of the water back again from off the earth they were left behind on land."

Not everyone looked at fossils the way Dr. Woodward did, however. Leonardo da Vinci disputed the Deluge theory. As an engineer building canals through stratified (layered) rock in northern Italy, he and his laborers turned up many marine fossils—oysters, snails, clams, and crabs. Da Vinci concluded from his finds that the fossils had not been deposited by a single flood but that they were the relics of an age when ocean water had covered that part of the earth.

In 1779, French naturalist Georges-Louis Leclere de Buffon took fossils into account in discussing the formation of the earth in his *Epochs of Nature*. Buffon noted that fossil shells were abundant in every part of the earth. He reasoned, therefore, that at one time the sea must have covered all the land. The fossils were the remains of creatures that lived in the sea and that were left on land when the waters receded. These early creatures were often quite unlike those that appeared later on the earth. Buffon thought that it would be possible to study the history of the species that succeeded each other by making a thorough study of fossils.

Another French naturalist, Jean-Baptiste de Lamarck, wrote a series of *Reports on the Fossils in the Vicinity of Paris* (1802–1806), which is considered to be a model of accurate scientific writing. He performed classification studies of both living and fossil mollusks.

As scientists built upon this early work with fossils, they found that fossils provided an important basis for dividing geologic time.

Fossilization Processes

When a plant or animal dies it may be eaten by other living animals. If it is not eaten, it will probably decay through bacterial and chemical action. And if either of these things happens, it will not be a fossil.

But if a plant or animal is buried quickly after death in mud, sand, or stagnant or brackish water, air cannot get to it and the usual decay processes do not take place. Freezing will also ward off decay. If a dead organism can escape both being eaten and total decay over the course of time, it will become a fossil.

The most common kinds of fossils are various marine-animal shells. Fossil hunters are most likely to find them in limestone or shale beds, especially where these are exposed on weathered slopes. During fossilization the shells were replaced by calcite or even quartz. Shell fossils may stand out on a slope or may even be perched on pedestals like golf balls on tees.

Relics from the plant kingdom, leaf fossils are found as impressions between two layers of shale. To find them, you must split the shale sheets apart. One of the best places to find leaf fossils is in shale strata that overlie coal beds.

Land animals have left fossil remains, too. Since land animals apparently did not develop until relatively late in the earth's history, the number and variety of their fossils is much smaller than those of sea animals. Residents of western North America, however, can find pieces of dinosaur bones, mammal teeth, and fossil footprints of various kinds.

■■■

The Burgess shale in Jasper National Park, Alberta, Canada, has yielded fossils of soft-bodied creatures. Some of them contained stomach contents from the animals' last meal.

■■■

Unaltered Preservation

Quick burial in sediments, usually under water, is the most common route to fossilization. The sediments then *lithify,* or turn to rock. In some cases, the hard parts of buried creatures survive virtually intact—like teeth, shells, and sometimes bones or other hard materials. The calcium-carbonate shell material of many marine invertebrates is easily preserved in an unaltered form. These *unaltered fossils* have not been changed from their original condition.

Permineralization

Some shells and most bones and plants are porous—that is, there are air spaces between the solid materials. When mineral matter carried in solution in groundwater is deposited into these air spaces, the fossil is *permineralized.* Permineralized fossils are heavier than comparable shells, bones, or plants in their normal state. Minerals that commonly fill the spaces of permineralized fossils are calcite, silica, and pyrite.

Replacement

Replacement fossils differ from permineralized fossils in that the groundwater dissolves the fossil organism and minerals—mainly silica and sometimes iron compounds—replace the organism molecule by molecule. The internal structures of replacement fossils are beautifully preserved. In petrified wood, for example, growth rings and cell structures are still visible.

Molds

A fossil impression called a *mold* occurs when groundwater seeps through the sediment containing a buried organism. If the water is weakly acidic, it dissolves shells and other hard parts containing the minerals calcite and aragonite. When the fossil is completely dissolved, an impression of the original material is left behind in the sedimentary rock. Molds of leaves and other very thin structures are called *imprints*.

Casts

A *cast* is formed when sediments and/or different minerals fill a fossil mold and produce an exact copy of the exterior of the original fossil.

Carbonization

Leaves and soft-bodied animals such as fish are sometimes preserved as thin films of carbon remaining in the rock. This process, called *carbonization,* has produced beautifully detailed fossil fern leaves.

Freezing

No matter how quickly creatures are buried in sediments, their fleshy parts usually rot away before fossilization of the hard parts occurs. Under unusual circumstances, however, plants and animals have been preserved as fossils when suddenly frozen. Frozen carcasses of mammoths, for instance, have been uncovered from the tundra of Siberia and Alaska.

Entrapment in Amber

Insects encased in amber are also fossils. These insects were trapped inside tree resin, which then hardened and was preserved as a fossil. Since the amber itself is a fossil, finds in amber are actually double fossils. Most amber is found along the Baltic Sea.

Entrapment in Natural Asphalt

One of the richest fossil sites is at Rancho La Brea, California—the famous La Brea Tar Pits. These tar pits have yielded fossilized remains of more than a million animals that were trapped in pools of natural asphalt formed by seepage from petroleum deposits.

Fossil Fuels

Coal and oil are classified as fossil fuels because they are the remains of ancient plants and animals.

Finding Fossils

About 99 percent of all fossils are found in sedimentary rock. Fossils do not occur in plutonic (intrusive) igneous rock, and they occur only rarely in extrusive igneous rock when ash falls and cooler lava flows literally buried plants or animals alive. Occasional blurred and distorted fossil traces occur in metamorphic rock like marble, but the process of metamorphism acting upon sedimentary rock usually destroys any fossils that may have been present.

It is possible for any sedimentary rock to contain fossils, but certain sedimentary formations contain many specimens while others have practically none. The most common sedimentary rocks containing fossils are shale, sandstone, and limestone. But not all shale, sandstone, and limestone contain fossils. Those that were laid down in a marine (saltwater) environment are the best prospects for fossil hunting. If you can locate marine sandstone, shale, or limestone, chances are favorable that you will find fossils.

You may have fossils hiding in your backyard or around the corner. You may be able to find fossils in a driveway or parking lot if it is lined with limestone. Or you may have to travel a distance to hunt them.

Because most rock layers are covered with loose material like sand and gravel called regolith, you need to find areas from which the regolith has been removed. The best places to look are fresh exposures of rock. Natural exposures of sedimentary rock occur where a stream has cut down through the regolith and into the bedrock. Other good exposures can be road cuts, mine dumps, quarries, and construction sites.

Caution: All of these places can be dangerous. Work with at least one other responsible person. Watch for traffic at road cuts. Always get permission to enter private property and follow any instructions you are given. Always beware of falling rocks.

Note: On some public lands, like parks or forests, fossil-collecting permits are required. Many parks, forests, and other publicly managed areas do not allow fossil collecting at all. Find out about the regulations before you begin collecting.

In natural exposures, good fossil specimens are frequently weathered out of the bedrock. These may be found where thin layers of soil overlie the bedrock and in accumulations of rocks that have weathered and fallen or slid from a cliff.

You can purchase fossils from local rock shops, from mail-order science catalogs, and at museum gift shops. Some companies sell fossil reproductions, also. One of them is Dino Productions of Englewood, Colorado. Their address is listed under "Science Supplies" in the Appendix.

Maps

Maps are essential for fossil hunters. The right maps will show you topography, local roads, sedimentary rock beds and outcrops, and even fossil-rich areas.

Local road maps or county maps usually show back roads that are too small to appear on state road maps. Sometimes local maps are printed in telephone directories. County maps are sold in bookstores and some grocery, convenience, and department stores. Your local automobile association office may carry county or local area maps. Check with county government or county commissioners' offices to see whether local maps are available. Sometimes they are distributed through automobile title and license bureaus.

Topographic maps for the entire United States are produced by the U.S. Geological Survey (USGS). They show terrain, land and water features, vegetation cover, and man-made structures. (See Chapter 3 for more about topographic maps.) You can obtain topographic map pricing information and indexes by state by contacting the USGS. For Canadian topographical maps, contact the Canada Map Office. Both addresses are listed in the "Finding Maps" section of the Appendix.

Geological maps are invaluable to fossil hunters, rock hounds, and gem collectors as well as the geologists and engineers they are designed for. Geological maps show distribution of exposed rocks and loose material at the earth's surface. They also make it possible to determine subsurface characteristics such as size, shape, and position of rock masses along with mineral deposits, fluids, or openings in the rock. Like topographic maps, geological maps use symbols, colors, and patterns. Geological maps, however, are more complex because they record information about rocks and their spatial relationships; sequence, thickness, geological structure, and history of rock formations; and the significant geological relationships of an area.

The USGS produces many kinds of geological maps:

- Quadrangle maps (four-sided areas)
- Mineral-resource maps
- Oil and gas maps
- Hydrologic maps (water distribution and movement)
- Geological reconnaissance maps of Antarctica

The quadrangle and mineral-resource maps are of greatest interest to fossil hunters.

The USGS's National Atlas Program has also produced national maps called "Geology," which show distribution of sedimentary, volcanic, and intrusive (plutonic) rock, and maps called "Surficial Geology," which show distribution of transported, untransported, and other surface deposits.

For more information on geological maps and the National Atlas Program, contact the USGS Map Distribution Center (the address is listed in the "Finding Maps" section of the Appendix).

In Canada, geological maps are available from the Geological Survey of Canada, which also offers pamphlets and posters on fossils in general and on fossils of the Burgess shale in Jasper National Park. You can contact the Geological Survey of Canada at the address listed in the "Finding Maps" section of the Appendix.

In addition, most state governments have divisions or departments of geological survey or natural resources that publish and sell state geological maps. State bureaus of mines may be another source.

If you're interested in dinosaur fossils, Dino Productions (their address is listed in the "Science" section of the Appendix) carries information on fossil hunting in the western states and produces maps showing surface rocks from the age of dinosaurs. Their series of state roadside geology books may also be helpful in locating sedimentary strata that could contain fossils.

Some natural history or geology museums have fossil societies. Joining one may be a good way to get in touch with others who share your interest, learn the best local fossil-hunting grounds, and perhaps even go on collecting trips. See the list of museums in the Appendix.

• •

PROJECT

Fossil Hunting

After choosing a fossil-hunting location, take your time to look over the area carefully. Look for surfaces where weathering may have exposed fossils. Break open larger rocks and especially concretions (nodular or irregular concentrations harder than the surrounding rock) if possible. If you locate any fossil you believe may be important or rare, like vertebrate bones, note its location and ask a professional (from a college, university, or museum) for help. Most professionals are willing to help because valuable finds are sometimes ruined by botched attempts to remove the fossils.

MATERIALS:

Tools for fossil collecting are similar to those used by any rockhound and are readily available in hardware stores if you don't already have them at home:

- Maps
- Compass
- Hammer (geologist's, plasterer's, or bricklayer's is best)
- Large and small stonecutter's chisels
- Collecting bag
- Notebook
- Pen(cil)
- Newspaper or other soft paper or cloth for wrapping specimens
- 10X hand lens or magnifying glass
- Hard hat
- Safety goggles
- Gloves
- First-aid kit
- Water and snacks (optional)

PROCEDURE:

Caution: Always wear protective equipment—hard hat, safety goggles, and gloves—when breaking and handling sharp rocks. Take a first-aid kit and beware of local hazards such as poisonous snakes. It's best to fossil hunt with another responsible person in case an emergency arises.

1. Use appropriate maps to locate a likely fossil-hunting area or ask other collectors for their recommendations.
2. Wear a hard hat to protect your head from possible falling rocks. Wear safety goggles to protect your eyes from possible flying rock particles. Wear gloves to protect your hands from sharp rocks.
3. When you find a fossil in a large rock—too large to carry—chisel a groove around the specimen, being careful to make the groove far enough away from the fossil so that it will not be damaged. Chisel deep enough to split the rock beneath the fossil and remove it intact.

   Note: Never try to trim a specimen closely in the field. Wait until you get home and can take your time to extract the fossil from the rock.

4. Wrap each fossil individually in newspaper, other soft paper, or cloth.
5. Wrap all specimens from the same location in a larger newspaper or cloth bundle.
6. Place a piece of paper containing a record of your find inside the larger bundle or make a separate record for each specimen. Include:

- Geographic location
- Location of the fossil in the rock formation
- Name and age of the rock formation, if known (geological maps may help)
- Characteristics of the exposed rock
- Relative abundance of fossils in the formation
- Variety of fossils in the formation

PROJECT

Fossil Preparation

Back at home or in the lab, you can trim and clean your fossil specimens. *Caution: Be sure to wear safety goggles.*

MATERIALS:

- Fossil specimens
- Safety goggles
- Gloves
- Water
- Small stonecutter's chisel
- Hacksaw
- Wire brush
- 10X hand lens or magnifying glass
- Shellac (optional)

PROCEDURE:

1. Wear safety goggles and gloves.
2. Use a hacksaw, if necessary, to saw through the rock surrounding a fossil specimen. Remove only small pieces of rock at a time.
3. Soak the fossil specimens in water for an hour or so to clean them and help soften the remaining rock material for easier removal.
4. When most of the surrounding rock has been removed, use a small chisel, ice pick, wire brush, or pliers to remove the remaining material. Electric-powered hobby tool sets often contain small drills and grinders that may make the task easier.
5. Use your 10X hand lens or magnifying glass to examine the fossil and make sure you've removed as much extra material as possible,

but not so much that it damages the fossil. You want to be able to study the fossil in detail.

6. Bones and other delicate fossils may need a coat of shellac as a protectant to prevent cracking and deterioration. If in doubt about whether to do this, check with the geology staff of a museum or university.

PROJECT

Identifying, Cataloging, and Storing Your Fossils

MATERIALS:

- Fossil specimens
- 10X hand lens
- Reference materials
- Heavy paper or lightweight cardboard
- Quick-drying, light-colored enamel
- Small paintbrush
- Fine-point permanent marker or india ink and pen
- Index cards
- Shoe box or other storage box (or empty egg cartons if specimens are small)
- Cardboard

PROCEDURE:

Identification

1. To identify fossils, compare your specimens with those described and pictured in reference books. You can obtain reference books from your local public library or nearby college or university library. Some natural history and geological museums maintain reference libraries. Check to see what the requirements are for using their facilities; membership is often required. State geological survey offices, located in state capitals, may have a list of publications relating to fossils that are tailored to the area where you obtained your specimens. These publications are usually excellent sources of information. And if you find a very good fossil, you may want to report your find to the geology department of the

nearest college or university, to your state geological survey, or to a nearby natural history museum.

2. When you have determined the name of each fossil specimen, label it. Make a label from good-quality paper or lightweight cardboard. This label will be stored with the fossil.

3. Use a permanent fine-point marker or india ink and a pen and include the following information on each label:
   - Identity of specimen
   - Name of the rock formation where the fossil was found
   - Geographic location of find
   - Geological age
   - Date of find (optional)
   - Sources used for identification (optional)
   - Any other information you can supply about the specimen or the find (optional)

Cataloging

1. Place a small spot of quick-drying enamel in an inconspicuous spot (like the back side) on each specimen.

2. Label each specimen with a number. Use a permanent marker or india ink to write a number on the spot of enamel on each fossil.

3. On an index card (use one card for each sample) or sheet of paper, record the following:
   - Specimen number
   - Identity of specimen
   - Name of the rock formation where the fossil was found
   - Geographic location of find
   - Geological age
   - Date of find
   - Sources used for identification
   - Any other information you can supply about the specimen or the find
   - Collector's name (You!)

   Catalog all your fossil specimens in this way.

Storage

Storing fossils is easy compared with storing other scientific collections. All you need to start are shoe boxes with homemade cardboard dividers. If your fossil specimens are small, you can use empty egg cartons. Label the boxes according to a system that you devise, such as one box for plant fossils, another for animal fossils. The important thing is to arrange your specimens so that you can find what you want when you want it. Make sure your labels are stored with each fossil. As you accumulate fossils, metal cabinets with divided drawers of various depths are ideal for storage.

PROJECT

Making Your Own "Fossils"

If you can't go out hunting fossils, you can make your own pseudofossils. You can make a tracking pit in a corner of your yard or outside your building. Be sure to get permission first.

Fossil Tracks

MATERIALS:

- Area of ground about 1 foot square
- Small shovel or spade
- Water
- Plaster of paris
- Plastic sandwich bag
- Unbreakable container to carry water

PROCEDURE:

1. Remove all vegetation from an area of land about 1 foot square so that only soil remains.
2. Water the soil until it becomes mud. This is your tracking pit.
3. Leave the pit alone overnight.
4. The next day, look in your tracking pit for small footprints left by animals that walked across it. These are your fossil molds.
5. Now make a fossil cast. Fill a plastic sandwich bag about $1/8$ to $1/4$ full with dry plaster of paris.
6. Put water in a small unbreakable container and go out to your tracking pit.
7. Pour enough water from the container into the sandwich bag to mix the plaster of paris to the consistency of thick soup.
8. Pour the plaster of paris onto the track molds and wait until the

plaster hardens. The time will be determined by how wet both the soil and the plaster are.

9. When the plaster has hardened, remove it from the soil mold and wash the dirt off. You now have a fossil cast.
10. Identify the footprints.

If you're a camper, try this project when you travel. You'll have a collection of casts from a variety of animals.

Indoor Fossils

If you don't have access to a spot of ground, you can make your own "fossils" in your room.

MATERIALS:
- Empty, rinsed ½-gallon (1.89-liter) paper milk carton or plastic bowl
- Scissors or knife
- Soil or modeling clay
- Water
- Plaster of paris
- Small sandwich bag
- Petroleum jelly (optional)

PROCEDURE:
1. Cut a ½-gallon (1.89-liter) paper milk carton off about 2 inches above the bottom, or use a plastic margarine container or other plastic bowl.
2. Fill the bottom of the milk carton or container with soil or modeling clay.
3. If you use soil, water it until it becomes stiff mud.
4. Have your pet put its paw in the mud or clay. If you don't have a pet, use your fingers to make a track. You can also press organic objects such as shells or leaves into the mud or clay to make impressions. Remove the objects.
5. Let the mud or clay harden. This is your fossil mold.
6. When the mold is firm, you may want to put a thin coat of petroleum jelly on it to make it easier to remove the cast.
7. Fill a plastic sandwich bag about ⅛ to ¼ full with dry plaster of paris.
8. Pour enough water into the sandwich bag to mix the plaster of paris to the consistency of thick soup.

9. Pour the plaster of paris onto the mold and wait until the plaster hardens. The time will be determined by how wet both the mud or clay and the plaster are.

10. When the plaster has hardened, remove it from the mold and wash off any dirt. You now have a fossil cast.

Activity

If you live in or near a large city, read about finding fossils in building stone in Chapter 17, "Urban Geology." Walk around the city and see how many fossils you can find and identify in the stone used to face buildings. This is a good project to do with a friend or two.

If you're a persistent fossil hunter, don't be surprised if you one day find an unusual fossil. It may be one that you can't identify. It may be one that is not generally found in the rock layer where you found it. It may be one that puzzles even a skilled paleontologist. Your find may help answer questions about the past. Remember that amateur paleontologists (like you!) have made many significant fossil discoveries.

Chapter Fifteen

Messengers from Space
··

Meteorites

What comes from space yet can be found almost anywhere on earth? About thirty-five hundred arrive each year. They can be very expensive but few people are familiar with them.

Need a hint? They are a kind of rock but are usually heavier than ordinary rocks. In dust form they are a component of soil.

Meteorites!

Meteorites are not the easiest rocks to find; only about twenty-five are documented each year. On the average, however, there is one meteorite per square mile, and their numbers are constantly increasing since these aliens continue to head for our planet.

So few meteorites are found because most people aren't looking for them and don't know what they look like. Even if they did, another problem is that many meteorites strongly resemble ordinary rocks found on the earth's surface. In fact, you may have picked one up and tossed it away as just another rock.

If you're lucky, though, you might just find that one has landed in your yard. A resident of Westlake, Ohio (a suburb of Cleveland), for instance, recently found a meteorite in his small garden. Back in 1983, treasure hunters in Florida who were looking for gold and silver found a 24-pound (10.9-kilogram) stony meteorite instead.

Meteoritic dust and micrometeorites may be easier to find, since they are more widespread, but you'll need a 10X hand lens to see them.

What Are Meteorites, Meteors, and Meteoroids?

As soon as a meteor or fragments of it land on earth it becomes a *meteorite*. Many astronomers feel meteorites are stray material from comets or asteroids, but they may also have come from Mars or our moon.

So what's a *meteor*? It is a body from space that has entered the earth's atmosphere. During its fall toward earth, it is heated by friction until it burns with a bright, visible light. Meteors, or "shooting stars," appear as bright streaks or flashes of light in the nighttime sky. They may be seen on almost any clear night and are usually more common after midnight. The best times for meteor watching are from midnight to dawn. The best place to view "shooting stars" is from an open country field, since city lights or a brightly lighted area may obscure them. Generally, you can see about ten per hour!

Meteors enter the earth's atmosphere at speeds from 25,000 to 75,000 miles per hour (40,000 to 120,000 kilometers per hour). At this speed, a body over 350 net tons (315 metric tons) will explode.

On just about any night, *sporadic* meteors fall out of the sky from any direction. These probably originate in the asteroid belt. At certain times of the year, meteors are more numerous; in fact, they fall in *meteor showers*. Shower meteors travel in groups called *swarms* and appear to be the remains of comets. They may originate from dust trails that comets leave behind. When a trail crosses earth's orbit, some of the dust particles enter our atmosphere and burn up as meteor showers. Showers occur at the same time year after year and appear to come from particular parts of the sky.

Meteor showers are named for constellations because the showers seem to radiate from points in certain constellations. For example, those that seem to come from Orion are Orionids; those from Gemini are Geminids.

■■

A SAMPLING OF METEOR SHOWERS:

Name	Date
Lyrid	April
Upsilon Pegasid	early August
Perseid	August
Draconid	October
Leonid	about November 16

■■

Although meteor showers appear to come from their namesake constellations, this is an illusion. Shower meteors actually travel in parallel lines. They only appear to radiate from a central area, just as snowflakes appear to do when we see them through an automobile's windshield.

Where do meteors come from? Will they ever end? A meteor in space (outside the earth's atmosphere) is called a *meteoroid.* Our solar system has untold millions of meteoroids, and perhaps they exist far beyond the solar system. Meteoroids may originate from the planets, moons of the planets, comets, or asteroids.

That is why scientists refer to meteorites—the fragments that eventually hit the ground—as "messengers from space." They have also been called the poor man's space probes because they come to us. They provide information about the other planets, comets, or asteroids that can be studied firsthand. When you hold a meteorite, you're holding a piece of another world.

Do meteors cause problems in the earth's atmosphere? In recorded history, meteors have not been a problem—but they could be. The National Aeronautics and Space Administration (NASA) is concerned about meteors colliding with spacecraft. It is also possible that a meteor could hit a high-flying jet. To date it hasn't happened, though.

How about collisions on earth? Although once in a great while we hear of a meteorite puncturing someone's roof or falling on a car, as yet no one has ever been killed by a meteorite. Mrs. Hewlett Hodges of Sylacauga, Alabama, came close, however. On November 30, 1954, while napping on her couch, Mrs. Hodges was hit on the hip by an 8-pound (3.6-kilogram) meteorite that crashed through the roof.

In November 1982, a 6-pound (2.7-kilogram) stony meteorite crashed through the roof of the Donahue family's home in Wethersfield, Connecticut, and landed under a dining room table. In October 1992, a meteorite smashed through the trunk of a car on the east coast of the United States.

Meteorites—those meteor fragments that reach the ground—vary in size from pieces hardly larger than dust particles to chunks weighing many tons. They may be nearly any shape. The average meteorite is estimated to weigh around 0.005 ounce (0.14 gram). According to the Center for Meteorite Studies at Arizona State University, the average person is most likely to find a meteorite that measures from 2 inches (5 centimeters) to 2 feet (0.61 meters) across.

The Hoba meteorite, found near Grootfontein, Namibia, is the largest known meteorite. It weighs about 60.5 short tons (55 metric tons). The second-largest known meteorite is the Cape York or Ahnighito meteorite found near Cape York on Greenland's west coast. Native people had used pieces of it to make weapons and tools before the explorer Robert E. Peary excavated it in 1897. He shipped it to New York City, where it is displayed in the Arthur Ross Hall of Meteorites at the American Museum of Natural History. It weighs 59 net tons (53.1 metric tons).

Figure 15-1. The Cape York (Ahnighito) iron meteorite on display in the Arthur Ross Hall of Meteorites at the American Museum of Natural History in New York City.

Meteor Craters

What happens when a large meteor collides with the earth (besides the fact that it then becomes a meteorite)? The collision will leave some kind of mark in the ground. If the impact is great enough, it will form a meteor crater.

The largest known crater believed to have been produced by a meteor was discovered in 1950 in northern Quebec, Canada. The New Quebec Crater consists of a circular pit 2.16 miles (3.6 kilometers) in diameter and 594 feet (180 meters) deep. The crater contains a lake surrounded by concentric piles of shattered granite. This crater is so large that it is not recognizable as a crater when viewed from the ground. Only from the air can you see its round crater shape.

An excellent example of a meteorite impact crater is Meteor Crater near Winslow, Arizona. You can stand on Meteor Crater's rim and see its characteristic crater shape. It is about 4,274 feet (1,295 meters) in diameter and 574 feet (174 meters) deep. Scientists estimate that this meteor-earth collision blew out 400 net tons (360 million metric tons) of rock from the earth.

MORE METEOR CRATER FACTS:

- More than 120 meteor craters have been identified worldwide.
- About 20 meteor craters have been identified in Canada.
- Diameters of known meteor craters range from 150 meters (500 feet) on up.

Meteoritic Dust

Even though large meteorites or meteorite craters are not common, the earth is subject to a constant barrage of meteoric "rain"—material that falls like dust and leaves no craters. Many of the meteors that shoot across the sky are reduced to fine dust by the heat generated by friction as they enter the earth's atmosphere. As fine dust, the meteor residue settles slowly toward the earth and becomes uniformly distributed.

This fine meteoritic dust is nearly everywhere—even indoors—but how can you find it? If you live in an area that does not contain igneous rocks, you're in luck. Try the following activity.

PROJECT

Finding Meteoritic Dust

This activity may help you find meteoritic dust particles—if you're in an area without igneous rock. Unfortunately, if you live in an area that contains igneous rock, it will be impossible to tell the meteoritic dust from igneous-rock dust particles that also have magnetic properties.

MATERIALS:

- Several samples of dust from around your home—inside or outside. This can be a thin layer from the top of the soil or, yes, even the "dust bunnies" under your bed.
- Flat dish or plate
- Bar magnet or other strong magnet
- 10X hand lens

PROCEDURE:

1. Collect several samples of dust and place them on the flat dish or plate.
2. Run the bar magnet or other type of strong magnet along the top of the dust. Make sure it is not static electricity that is making the dust magnetic.
3. If the magnet picks up some small pieces of dust, that dust could be meteoritic.
4. Look at the dust the magnet picked up under the magnification of a 10X hand lens. Is it dark or light in color? If it is dark as well as magnetic, it is more likely to have come from space.

● ●

Meteors, Meteorites, and Mass Extinction

Are you wondering, "What's the point? Why look for meteoritic dust?" Do your friends look at you strangely when you tell them you're looking for meteoritic dust?

Ask them what they know about the Cretaceous extinction theory proposed by Luis and Walter Alvarez. It sent the world's scientific community into turmoil. It's the theory that dinosaurs were killed off by an asteroid or a comet about 65 million years ago.

It started in 1978 when Walter Alvarez, a geologist from the University of California at Berkeley, was studying a thin layer of clay in a deep gorge near Gubbio, Italy. Gubbio is a tiny medieval village halfway between Rome and Florence. The reddish clay layer that Walter was examining was only half an inch (1.27 centimeters) thick. But this half-inch-thick clay bed divided the Cretaceous time period (the time during which dinosaurs lived) and the Tertiary time period (the period after the dinosaurs lived).

Walter wanted to know how long it took for the half inch of clay to be deposited. If he knew that, he would know how long it took for the dinosaurs to die off and become extinct.

Walter took this problem to his father, Luis Alvarez, who had won a Nobel Prize in physics for studies on subatomic particles. Although Luis had only one geology course in college, as a physicist he had an idea about determining how long it took for the clay to be laid down. His idea had to do with meteorites. Here it is in his own words.

When meteorites enter the atmosphere, most of them burn up—they're shooting stars. When they burn up they turn into meteoric dust and the dust settles down on the surface of the earth. It's just as though you went around with a salt shaker and shook meteoric dust all over the earth at a certain constant rate. So my basic idea was that you could tell how fast the clay layer was laid down by observing how much this special kind of salt, if you will, was sprinkled all over the earth by the meteoric dust coming down.

Luis Alvarez didn't use a magnet running over the soil to attract the meteoritic dust like we would do. Rather, he used the rare element iridium. He measured the amount of iridium in the clay layer. You see, most iridium on earth is in the earth's core. Meteorites, however, contain around 10,000 times more iridium than native earth rocks. So the iridium would tell Luis how much meteoritic dust was in the clay. That would tell him how long it took nature to lay down the clay stratum and thus how long it took for the dinosaurs to die out.

Frank Asaro and Helen Michel, two physical chemists, measured the iridium in the clay and found that it contained about 30 times more iridium than could be explained by meteoric dust landing on earth. Then they checked the iridium levels between the Cretaceous and Tertiary periods and found 160 times the normal level in a sea cliff in Denmark.

Actually, it took Luis Alvarez weeks of thinking about all the possibilities that might have caused these high iridium levels before he finally came up with the idea that an asteroid or comet could have collided with the earth. The impact would have shot great quantities of dust up into the atmosphere, from which it rained down on the land, giving these narrow layers high iridium levels. The dust cloud would also have blocked out the sunlight, causing the earth's surface temperature to drop. The decreased temperatures, lack of sunlight, and climate changes would eventually have killed off all the dinosaurs as well as some of the other plants and animals on earth.

Since 1980, when Luis and Walter Alvarez suggested their theory, geologists have been searching for the crater that such a great asteroid would have made. The geologists are looking on land as well as under lakes and oceans. They have found forty craters in the United States and Canada, but they are either the wrong age or the wrong size to fit the Alvarezes' theory.

A great problem in locating craters is the restless nature of our planet. Erosion and weathering destroy the craters. Glaciers that in times past covered most of Canada and part of the United States have filled in and flattened craters. The drifting plates of the earth's crust that cause mountain ranges to form also destroy topographic features. Rain, wind, and flooding can wash away or fill in craters.

For instance, Meteor Crater in Arizona is about twenty-five thousand years old. It has about 100 feet (30 meters) of sediment built up in its bottom. If that happened in twenty-five thousand years, think of the amount of weathering, erosion, and deposition that must have occurred in the 65 million years since the last dinosaur roamed the earth and therefore affected older craters.

But Luis Alvarez wasn't finished thinking. After examining all the information about the earth's craters, Alvarez theorized that about every 26 million years a large object from space hits our planet and forms a crater or cluster of craters, resulting in mass extinction.

Do you agree with Luis and Walter Alvarez? If you do, that's fine. If you don't, you've got lots of company. The Alvarezes' theory is far from winning total acceptance by all scientists.

"You'd be surprised how many scientists were simply scandalized by the very thought of mass extinction being caused by the impact of a large object," Luis Alvarez commented. "I think probably a lot of people just don't like to think that big rocks can fall out of the sky."

All this controversy has been caused—and hundreds, if not thousands, of books and articles have been written—around the world just because someone was looking for meteoric dust. A little curiosity can spawn new theories, stun the scientific world, and change the way we look at the past.

Meteorite Hunting

Want to try for bigger meteorites? Great! You have the spirit of an adventurer, a scientist, and a treasure hunter. "A treasure hunter?" you ask. Yes, some of the rare stony-iron meteorites have brought in over $100 an ounce. Iron meteorites average under $25 per ounce; stony meteorites range somewhere between these extremes. And they can be found any-where on earth.

Before you get too excited, though, remember that only a handful are found each year. Good hunting!

■■

Should you find a meteorite, who owns it? The owner of the land is legally the owner of any meteorites found on it, although you could negotiate a deal with the property owner. In the case of state-owned property, the state is the legal owner. It is essential to obtain permission before beginning your meteorite hunt on private property.

■■

Whether or not you receive money for a meteorite, hunting these vistors from space is fun and rewarding. Of course, you'll want to know what you're looking for when you're meteorite hunting. There are three main categories of meteorites:

- Stony
- Stony-iron
- Iron

The composition of each reveals a different history. *Stony* meteorites are the most common, yet are one of the hardest to recognize since they are similar in appearance to many natural rocks on earth. Stony meteorites contain about 75 to 90 percent silicates, and some contain large amounts of carbonlike materials. The other 10 to 25 percent is nickel-iron and iron sulfide. The best way to find stony meteorites is to look in an area where a fall was observed. After a few years the stony meteorites are affected by weathering and are not distinguishable from terrestrial rocks.

Some stony meteorites probably condensed from the gaseous solar nebulas that formed the planets. Another kind of stony meteorite contains carbon interspersed with organic molecules. Recently found examples contain complex amino acids and primitive diamonds. A third type of stony meteorite has a structure similar to earth's basalt rocks. They probably formed at or near the surface of the small planetary bodies in the asteroid belt.

Stony-iron meteorites are the rarest type. They contain crystals of rock embedded in metal or rock and metal more or less blended together. They are composed equally of silicates and the metallic iron-nickel alloys along with traces of other minerals. *Pallasites* are the most abundant of these rare stony-iron types. They are also the most attractive since they contain crystals of the greenish silicate mineral olivine embedded in a matrix of nickel-iron. They were probably formed between the core and mantle of their parent bodies.

Iron meteorites are composed almost entirely of iron and nickel or nickel-iron alloy. They make up a large percentage of meteorite finds because iron meteorites are more resistant to weathering. Iron meteorites:

- are black in color,
- contain shiny metallic masses,
- have warty surfaces,
- are usually magnetic, and
- are prone to rust.

It is interesting that even though meteorites are visitors from another world and over thirty chemical elements have been found in these alien rocks, no unfamiliar substance has been found in them.

■■■■■■■■■■■■■■■■■■■■■■■■■■■■■■■■■■■■

MORE METEORITE FACTS

- The Hoba meteorite measures about 9 feet (2.7 meters) by 8 feet (2.4 meters).
- Both the Hoba and Cape York (Ahnighito) meteorites are the nickel-iron type.
- In 1976, a nickel-iron meteorite weighing 2,758 kilograms (6,068 pounds) was found in California's Old Woman Mountains.
- The largest piece of stony meteorite recovered weighs 1,756 kilograms (3,902 pounds). It was part of a shower that struck Jilin (formerly Kirin), China, on March 8, 1976.
- The Allende meteorite fall over Chihuahua, Mexico, on February 8, 1969, yielded meteorites dating back 4.61 million years.
- Every day, meteorites and meteoritic dust add 500 pounds (225 kilograms) to the earth's mass.
- Most large meteorites are believed to have come from asteroids.

■■■■■■■■■■■■■■■■■■■■■■■■■■■■■■■■■■■■

As a meteor falls through the atmosphere and breaks apart, the fragments shower to Earth over a specific geographical area, called a *strewn field*. The area is usually elliptical in shape.

On February 8, 1969, the Allende meteor blazed across the sky near Pueblito de Allende in Chihuahua, Mexico. After producing a series of sonic booms, the meteor broke apart and scattered several tons of debris.

About twenty-five new meteorites are discovered each year, of which only about six are classified as recently fallen. In North America, the states of Kansas, Texas, and New Mexico yield the most meteorite finds. Other prime regions for meteorite hunting are the deserts of Australia, Mexico, and Chile. Since about 1980, scientists have gathered many meteorites from the Antarctic ice fields. The dry, cold environment preserves meteorites extremely well. Some Antarctic meteorites are believed to have come from our moon and possibly from Mars.

Modern meteorite searchers often use metal detectors. Meteorite hunters also frequently search in locations where new meteorites may have fallen. From visual sightings of bright "shooting stars," the fall location can be estimated. A meteor photographed in 1977 led to the discovery of a meteorite at Innisfree, Alberta, eleven days after the meteor sighting.

One good place to hunt meteorites is in a farmer's rock pile. Another good site is a ravine alongside a field, because the farmer may have tossed rocks into the ravine.

One of the best ways to learn to recognize meteorites is to visit a museum or university that has a good collection. If you can't find a meteorite, the "Meteorite Dealers" section of the Appendix lists places from which you can order a meteorite to start your own collection.

The Geological Survey of Canada offers a free poster on meteorites. To contact them, see the "Finding Maps" section of the Appendix.

● ●

PROJECT

Searching for Alien Rocks

Going out to find a meteorite? You'll need a detective's attitude and a spirit of adventure. But don't forget common sense and safety. Even if it's only to a nearby park or the field across the road, always let a parent or other adult know where you're going and when you'll be back. If you're venturing farther, bring someone with you. You may want a camera loaded with film, a topographic map of the area, a pencil and notepad, a compass, and a first-aid kit. Be on the lookout for poisonous plants and animals.

If you think you've found a meteorite, photograph the area and write down the details:

• Date and time
• Location
• Size of hole or crater (if any)
• Surrounding soil or rock type

Excavate the suspected meteorite carefully and try to keep it intact.

Here are eight physical characteristics of meteorites to look for as you search in the field, backyard, or park.

1. Meteorites are usually dark in color.
2. If it is a very recent fall, the meteorite will have a black fusion crust; if it's an old fall, its exterior will be brown from rust.
3. Meteorites are usually very dense—that is, they will feel heavier than an average rock of the same size.
4. Most meteorites are very magnetic, even the stony types. (The exception is the stony carbonaceous chondrite type.) Few terrestrial rocks are magnetic. To check if your rock is magnetic, you can use a pocket compass. If the rock is magnetic, the compass needle will follow the rock as you move it around the compass.
5. A meteorite's surface is usually pitted. The pits are generally oval or elliptical and may look like thumbprints.
6. Meteorites are usually oblong in shape.

7. Most meteorites have curved edges; very few have sharp edges.
8. The rock is not porous and has no "bubble" holes. Meteorites are not porous and do not have bubbled surfaces.

If your sample passes these visual tests, here are some physical tests to perform before you submit your sample to a meteorite identification laboratory.

MATERIALS:

- Fingernail
- Penny
- Steel file or piece of glass
- Piece of string at least 12 inches (30.5 centimeters) long
- Magnet
- Spring scale or triple-beam balance
- Graduated cylinder (You can make your own from a bottle marked in cubic centimeters or milliliters.)
- Glass or jar filled with water
- Emery wheel or emery paper
- 10X hand lens

PROCEDURE:

1. Check the hardness of the rock. If it's a meteorite, it should be harder than your fingernail, harder than a penny, but softer than window glass or a steel file. That means neither your fingernail nor a penny can scratch the rock, but window glass or a steel file will scratch it. This test demonstrates hardness between 4 and 5 on the Mohs hardness scale.
2. Hang a magnet on a string and hold the string and magnet near your sample. If the rock attracts the magnet, it means the rock is magnetic. Again, most meteorites are magnetic.
3. Measure the density of your find. Density refers to mass per unit volume, and it is usually expressed as grams per cubic centimeter (g/cc). With rare exceptions, meteorites have a density of at least 3.3 g/cc.
   a. Using the scale or triple-beam balance, determine the mass of your specimen to the nearest tenth of a gram.
   b. Determine the volume of your specimen by water displacement. First, put some water in the graduated cylinder and read the water level. Then hang the specimen from a string into the water

in the graduated cylinder and read the water level again. From this amount, subtract the first reading to get your specimen's volume.

    c. Find density by dividing the volume into the mass.

4. Measure the specific gravity of your find. (Iron meteorites have a specific gravity of about 7.5.)

    a. Weigh the rock in the air. Tie the rock on a piece of string, then tie the other end of the string to the hook on the end of a spring scale or balance and record the rock's weight.

    b. Keep the rock hanging from the scale, but now let it hang into a glass or jar of water so the rock is completely covered with water and not touching the sides or bottom of the glass or jar. Record the rock's weight in water. The weight should be less than it was in air. (See Chapter 12, Figures 12-1 and 12-2.)

    c. Subtract the rock's weight in water from its weight in air. Divide that answer into the weight of the rock in air. This gives you the rock's specific gravity.

5. Grind a small area of the rock with an emery wheel or a piece of emery paper. Stony meteorites will show shiny flecks of bright metal, and they often have shiny veins running through them. Use a 10X hand lens to detect the flecks.

• •

Positive Meteorite Identification

If your find passes all these tests and meets the characteristics of a meteorite, you may submit a sample of it to the nearest meteorite identification laboratory. However, many labs require you first to write, describing your find.

The Center for Meteorite Studies at Arizona State University has prepared a checklist for suspected meteorites. If you can answer "yes" to all five questions, the object is very likely to be a meteorite. In some cases, some answers may be "no" and the object may still be a meteorite. If all answers are "no," the object is probably not a meteorite.

1. Is the specimen heavy?
2. Is the specimen solid and compact?
3. Is the specimen attracted by a magnet?
4. Is the specimen black or brown and rather smooth on the outside?
5. Does the specimen show metallic iron specks on a cut surface?

Here is a list of laboratories that will test suspected meteorites.

United States

Center for Meteorite Studies
Dr. Carleton B. Moore, Director
Arizona State University
Tempe, AZ 85287-2504.
(602) 965-6511

They will examine any specimen thought to be a meteorite free of charge and estimate its value. An offer of purchase will be made for any specimens proving to be meteorites. The center also offers the following suggestions: If you find a meteorite, "note carefully its location, take photographs of the meteorite and its location, then contact us." The center also offers a brochure on meteorite identification.

Field Museum of Natural History
Department of Geology
Roosevelt Road at Lake Shore Drive
Chicago, IL 60605-2496
(312) 922-9410

The Field Museum's Department of Geology has an active research program in meteoritics. They examine samples brought in by the public as suspected meteorites, but you must make an appointment in advance.

American Museum of Natural History
Dr. Martin Prinz, Curator of Meteorites
Central Park West at 79th Street
New York, NY 10024-5192
(212) 769-5000

Write for instructions before sending specimens.

Oklahoma Meteorite Laboratory Inc.
John R. Martin, Director
P.O. Box 1923
Stillwater, OK 74076
(405) 624-9816

They will examine specimens thought to be meteorites free of charge. Sufficient return postage must accompany each sample. An offer of purchase will be made for any specimens proving to be meteorites.

National Museum of Natural History
Smithsonian Institution
Division of Meteorites, NHB-119
14th and Constitution Avenue, NW
Washington, DC 20560
(202) 357-1300

They examine suspected meteorites free of charge, and the specimen remains the property of the owner. Write for guidelines.

Canada

Meteorite Identification
Geological Survey of Canada
601 Booth Street
Ottawa, Ontario
Canada K1A 0E8

England

The Museum of Natural History
Department of Mineralogy
Cromwell Road
London, England SW7 5BD
(071) 938-9123

They "identify suspected meteorites free of charge if only a limited amount of work is required. If a more detailed examination were needed we would either keep a sample if the object were a meteorite, or we would charge a fee if the object were of no interest to us. Normally we prefer to be sent a sample of a few grains in weight."

Australia

Western Australian Museum
Dr. Alex Bevan, Curator of Mineralogy and Meteoritics
Department of Earth and Planetary Sciences
Francis Street, Perth
Western Australia, 6000
(09) 328-4411

They have an active program of meteorite recovery and research and deal with several hundred recoveries per year. Write for more information.

If you're interested in the latest meteor sightings and activities of meteorite hunters, consider subscribing to *Meteor News,* a ten-page newsletter published four times a year. The annual subscription rate is $5.00 in the United States and $7.00 in Canada and other countries. A free sample copy is available upon request. Contact *Meteor News* at Route 3, Box 1062, Callahan, FL 32011.

Chapter Sixteen

Finding Fault
•••

"**Y**ou're always finding fault." Perhaps you've been corrected for frequently complaining about a sister's or brother's actions.

"You're always finding fault." Perhaps you've blurted this out to a friend who criticized you.

"You're always finding fault." Perhaps you've replied this way to parents who seem to expect perfection.

"You're always finding faults." Perhaps that's what one geologist said to the other geologist!

Geologic *faults* aren't imperfections or mistakes, however. They are fractures or breaks in rock along which movement or slippage occurred. (If no movement occurs along a break in rock, it is simply called a *joint*.) Movement along faults is usually slow, but in some cases movement is rapid enough to produce earthquakes.

Faults can be found anywhere, but are more abundant in mountainous areas. One of the best-known faults in the United States is the San Andreas Fault in California, which stretches northwest from the Imperial Valley for about 600 miles (970 kilometers) to Point Arena on California's northern coast. Not all faults are as immense or dramatic as the San Andreas. Some have displacements measured in miles or kilometers, but there are also innumerable small faults in the rock beneath our feet.

Sometimes when rock layers are subjected to the same stresses that cause faults they don't break but instead bend, creating *folds*. Folds are often visible in exposed rock layers along road cuts in hilly or mountainous regions. An upward fold in rock is called an *anticline,* and a downward fold in rock is called a *syncline.*

● ●

PROJECT

Folding the Earth's Crust

Rocks in the earth's crust will often fold and bunch up when they are slowly compressed horizontally. You can see this for yourself using a package of construction paper in which each colored sheet represents a different layer of rock.

MATERIALS:

• Package of multicolored construction paper

PROCEDURE:

1. Remove the construction paper from its packaging.
2. Grasp the stack of construction paper at each end.
3. Push your hands together slowly to compress the paper.
4. Notice how the paper bends and folds much like the earth's crust does.

You can also do this simple project with three or more pieces of different-colored modeling clay arranged in thin layers on top of one another. Push the ends of the clay layers toward the center.

● ●

There are many kinds of faults. They are classified according to the type and direction of movement that has occurred. The surface along which fault movement occurs is called the *fault plane,* even though the fault surface is irregular, not entirely planar.

Often, one surface of the fault will be above the other. The rock wall overlying this type of fault is called the *hanging wall,* and the underlying rock wall is called the *footwall.*

• In *normal* faults, the hanging wall apparently moved down compared to the footwall.
• In *reverse* faults, the hanging wall apparently moved up compared to the footwall.
• *Thrust* faults are reverse faults with low angles, allowing one rock mass to thrust over the other.

- In *lateral* faults, rock on each side of the fault slipped past rock on the other side without raising or lowering.

For more descriptions of other, more-complicated fault types, visit your local library and consult a geology reference work. Faults with appreciable movement are shown on geologic maps. Small fault displacements are usually ignored in mapping because they would be imperceptible at the scale of the map. But if the offset is large enough to be mappable, the fault is shown.

Figure 16-1. Faults along a river wall, Big Bend National Park, Texas.

Activity
Look for folds and faults in exposed rock layers along a river or stream or a highway cut. Locate anticlines and synclines of folds.

Notice how strata on either side of a fault may be offset. If possible, measure the offset.

If you have a camera, photograph the folds and/or faults.

Caution: Wear appropriate clothing and sturdy shoes. Be especially careful of traffic at road cuts. Go with another responsible person.

Note: Always get permission before entering private property.

Finding faults (and folds) is not difficult when you know what to look for.

Chapter Seventeen

Urban Geology
••

G eology! When we hear that word we may first think of majestic mountains like the Rockies or even the Appalachians. Or we may think of volcanoes or earthquakes. We may picture scientists setting up camp in a remote location with rocky cliffs and outcrops that they will spend weeks studying and sampling. Generally, the word *geology* brings a faraway place to mind.

Unless they live in a geologically renowned area, people don't think about local geology. "There's no geology around here," you may say to yourself. Well, take a closer look. Ordinary cities and towns are geologically interesting.

Think about the construction process. Project engineers must consider things like soil, bedrock, and seismic characteristics. Think of the soil profiles and rock strata that may be visible at excavation sites.

Now think of completed buildings and the earth materials that may have been used in their construction: stone like granite, limestone, sandstone, marble, and slate. Look at your own home's foundation. If it's an older building, native stone may have been used. For years, sidewalks were made from slate, sandstone, and even bricks formed from clay. Cobblestones of local origin were laid side by side to make roads. Now look up for a moment. Some buildings have slate shingles on their roofs. Now go inside. Perhaps you have a stone wall or fireplace inside your home. In some of these building stones you can even find fossils.

More and more people are interested in local geology. There may be organized urban geology hikes (often sponsored by a local museum) in your area to find examples of those things mentioned above. If not, get some interested friends together and take a walk around your neighborhood.

Building Stone

Building stone ranks with steel as an important construction material. Building stone can be used for the foundations, walls, and steps of buildings. It can also be used as supports for piers and bridges. Inside and outside, stone is used to finish and decorate buildings and bridges in a variety of ways.

Crushed Stone

The most common building stone in the United States is crushed stone. Because it's crushed and used as fill material, it's hard to study. Crushed stone is quarried stone, usually limestone, that is crushed or broken into small pieces, making it suitable for highways and industrial construction. In 1990, the United States used more than 1.2 billion short tons of crushed stone.

Dimension Stone

Dimension stone refers to stone in natural blocks or slabs that can be cut into definite shapes and sizes. This type of building stone is ideal to study. Good dimension stone (that is, with no structural flaws such as cracks) can be expected to last at least a hundred years and probably longer. Many stone buildings that were erected before the Revolutionary War are in excellent condition today. The first homes in your neighborhood may have been built of native stone, hand-cut from a nearby quarry or outcropping. If available nearby, sandstone and limestone were commonly used by early settlers.

The best dimension stone has the fewest pore spaces or air cells in it. The fewer the pore spaces, the better the stone can resist the wearing effects of weather. More pore spaces mean more places that water can get into the stone and freeze during cold weather. Because water expands when it freezes, it can create small cracks in the stone and make it easy for small pieces to chip off.

Common types of dimension stone are granite, limestone, sandstone, marble, and slate. In 1990, the United States used nearly 1.2 million short tons of dimension stone.

Identifying Rock Materials Used in Building

Identifying rocks used as building materials is much the same as identifying rock specimens you collect. However, you have to make your identification largely by sight and touch. You can't break the building stones apart, lift them, or see how they react to acid. See Chapters 12 and 13 for more on identification of rocks and minerals.

Granite

Granite is a common intrusive (formed inside the earth) rock that makes up the core of many mountain ranges. Granite contains the minerals orthoclase (potassium) feldspar, hornblende (amphibole), quartz, and mica. These minerals are visible as uniform-sized coarse grains or crystals that are usually pink, black, and white. However, in various areas around the world, the presence of small amounts of other minerals changes granite's color (to black, gray, and white, for instance). Granite can be highly polished and may be used this way for a variety of purposes, even including floors. It is widely used ornamentally because of its color variety, polishability, and resistance to weathering.

Is there a cemetery near you? Check the gravestones. Modern gravestones are made of polished granite, which is highly weather resistant. If there are old, worn stones in the cemetery, they are probably made of marble or sandstone. Since marble and sandstone are both more easily weathered than granite, decades of wind, rain, and acids carried with the rain combine to dissolve and remove the rock's surface little by little until you can no longer read the inscriptions on the gravestones.

Limestone

Most limestone is white or nearly white, but some is naturally gray or black and may resemble basalt. Weathering and airborne pollutants can also cause limestone to darken with age. In crushed form, limestone is often used as filler in highway and building construction and for stone driveways and parking lots.

Calcite is the chief mineral composing limestone, and limestone is one of the most abundant sedimentary rocks. Most limestone forms biochemically in the sea from the accumulated remains of marine organisms like algae, mollusks, and corals. This is why so many marine fossils are found in limestone. So if you find a building constructed with limestone blocks, you may be able to find fossils, too.

Travertine is a type of limestone formed in caves by the evaporation of mineral solutions rich in calcium carbonate. Travertine may be porous, in which case it is called *calcareous tufa*. The word *tufa* comes from the Italian for "soft rock" since this material is porous and has a spongy texture. Travertine is sometimes used inside buildings because it is sound absorbent as well as decorative.

Marble

Marble is a coarse-grained metamorphic rock produced by the action of heat and/or pressure on limestone or dolomite. Under tremendous heat and pressure, carbonates in the limestone dissolve bit by bit and recrystallize into larger grains. Pure marble is snow-white, but impurities produce a variety of colors. Marble used as building stone may be white, green, red, brown, or black, and many varieties of marble show intricate bandings and mottlings.

Marble, especially imported marble, was once the province of the wealthy and can often be found in mansions built years ago for rich industrialists in North America. Marble fireplaces, mantels, staircases, and sinks were common. Marble columns and other decorative features are also common inside public and private buildings, often in entryways and lobbies. Marble used on building exteriors is prone to deterioration from weathering, however.

Sandstone

Sandstone is composed of sand-sized particles ($1/16$ to 2 millimeters in diameter). Because it is distinguished by particle size, its mineral content varies. Varieties of sandstone include:

- *Quartz sandstone*—made up of sand-sized grains of quartz.
- *Arkose*—a sandstone composed mainly of sand-sized grains of feldspar and quartz.
- *Graywacke*—a dense sandstone containing rock fragments and clay particles.
- *Orthoquartzite*—a white sandstone made of quartz grains and cemented by quartz.
- *"Painted Desert" sandstone*—the color of the Painted Desert because the grains are held together by red iron-oxide cements.

Look for large sandstone blocks used as foundations and facings of older buildings and churches. Look for it in stone walks, where it was once commonly used. Feel it. Rub your fingers over it. It should feel gritty like sandpaper.

In addition to natural coloration, sandstone often blackens over time because of weathering and pollutants in the air.

Slate

Slate is a metamorphic rock formed from shale. The intense heat and/or pressure during metamorphism forces the clay minerals in shale into parallel alignment. Slate is usually dark gray, but it may be green if it contains an abundance of chlorite. Slate that is black contains iron sulfides or carbonaceous material.

The strong parallel alignment of slate's mineral crystals allows it to break into thin, flat sheets. These thin, flat sheets can then be used for roof tiles and walkway slabs. Slate was once commonly used for school chalkboards.

Man-Made Rock

Sandstone and limestone are not used in construction today to the extent they once were. Man-made materials like concrete and brick have replaced them. Because of their concentrated used in developed areas, these man-made building materials are sometimes referred to as *urbanite*. Perhaps that is what scientists of future civilizations will call these relics when they are unearthed. The varieties of urbanite are manufactured from natural earth materials, however.

Concrete

Concrete is the most widely used construction material in the world. In the United States, almost twice as much concrete is used as all other building materials combined.

Because it is pliable when wet, concrete can be formed and molded in a variety of ways and provides structural continuity, strength, and durability at a reasonable cost. Its surface can be textured or smoothed, colored or not colored. It can be made watertight or porous and permeable. It can be made to resemble brick or stone. Concrete, often reinforced with steel rods or mesh, is used in highways, bridges, dams, large and small buildings, homes, airport runways, sidewalks, irrigation structures, docks, silos, and even ships.

Although widespread use of concrete is a characteristic of modern life, concrete itself isn't new. Egyptians built concrete columns more than thirty-six hundred years ago that are still standing today. At the beginning of the Christian era almost two thousand years ago, many great Roman architectural works were constructed of concrete.

Concrete consists of a combination of sand, gravel, crushed stone, and slag, held together with portland cement (or gypsum plaster), which hardens and adheres when mixed with water.

Portland cement, first produced in England in 1845, is manufactured from lime-bearing materials such as limestone, clay, shale, or blast-furnace slag containing alumina and silica. The usual composition of portland cement is 60 percent lime, 19 percent silica, 8 percent alumina, 5 percent iron, 5 percent magnesia, and 3 percent sulfur trioxide. By varying these percentages or adding other components, portland cement's properties can be varied. When portland cement is mixed with water, its components react to form a cementing medium. In properly mixed concrete, each particle of sand and aggregate is surrounded and coated by this paste, which also fills spaces between the particles. As it sets and hardens, the materials are bound into a solid mass.

Because concrete contains sand and crushed limestone, you may be able to find shell fragments and even fossils in it.

Brick

Brick can be considered a man-made rock, too. And it's been around even longer than concrete. Brick was the chief building material of Mesopotamia and Palestine, places lacking wood and stone. About nine thousand years ago, the inhabitants of Jericho in Palestine built with brick. The Great Wall of China is constructed of brick. In the Americas, native civilizations built with sun-dried adobe brick. Warm, red, unglazed brick was brought to North America by early colonists.

Bricks are heat-hardened blocks of clay used for construction and decorative facings. Although bricks may be dried in the sun, they are more commonly baked in a kiln. The cost of bricks is relatively low, they resist dampness and heat, and can last longer than stone. The color of bricks varies with the types of clay used in their manufacture. Many bricks are the ordinary red ones that come to mind when we hear "brick." They've even given their name to a color—brick red. But bricks may also be yellow, black, gray, or pink. They may be textured and/or brilliantly glazed. Still other bricks are made of special fireclays for use in building ovens, stoves, and fireplaces. Blocks of glass may even be classified as bricks.

Glass

Glass is another common form of urbanite. It is made primarily of silica fused at high temperatures with borates or phosphates. Molten glass is cooled to a rigid state without crystallization taking place. When enough heat is applied, glass can reconvert to a liquid form. This makes glass recyclable. Glass can be transparent, translucent, or opaque. It can be made in an array of colors with the addition of small amounts of different chemicals.

Activity
Take time to look around your home or school and identify earth materials used in construction or for decorative effect. Document them with photos if you'd like.

PROJECT

Urban Geology Hunt

Join an organized city geology hike, or get an interested friend or two together and organize your own. Look for natural rocks, fossils, and man-made "urbanite."

Public buildings, churches, chapels, and temples are all good places to start looking. The exteriors of many of these buildings were built with native stone. Inside, various types of stone, sometimes imported, were probably used for decoration. You should be able to find examples of all three major rock types: igneous, sedimentary, and metamorphic. Many of these structures have exterior (and interior) pillars, cornerstones, or insets that differ from the main type of stone used in the building. Sometimes columns and stone from other structures were used to build new churches.

Note: It is wise to call ahead when visiting places of worship.

Here's an example of a variety of rock found in one structure.

Saint Ann's Church in Cleveland Heights, Ohio, was built of Salem Limestone from quarries in south-central Indiana. The Salem Limestone formation is from the Mississippian Age and is composed primarily of fossils, including sea-lily stems, bryozoan fronds, and trace fossils made by animal movements. Inside, Saint Ann's floors are pink marble, and the walls of beige limestone containing brachiopod fossils. Its columns of light beige limestone were obtained from a former bank building. The holy water fonts—formerly the bank's drinking fountains—are white marble with gray veining.

MATERIALS:

- Map of planned route
- Notebook
- Pen(cil)
- Camera with film (optional)

PROCEDURE:

1. Plan a route through your neighborhood, town, or several city blocks that includes a mix of newer and older buildings.

   Note: It's best to walk with a responsible friend. Be sure to let a parent or another adult know when and where you're going and when you plan to return. Always ask permission before entering private property.

2. Use a separate page in your notebook to record information about the geology of each of the structures listed in step 3. List things like:

   • Location
   • Approximate age of building or structure
   • Identification of rock or other building material
   • Whether the building material is natural or man-made
   • Visibility of fossils in limestone and sandstone
   • Whether stones are polished or rough, cut or used as found
   • Whether the building stones have been weathered

3. Look at the following structures:

   • Streets
   • Sidewalks
   • Building exteriors (check especially for decorative stone use)
   • Building interiors (if there is public access; check especially interior floors, columns, and decorative stone use)
   • Building roofs (where visible)
   • Cemetery gravestones
   • Monuments
   • Bridges
   • Other structures

4. If you find fossils in limestone and sandstone, describe them. Are they marine or land organisms? Can you identify them?

5. You may want to use a camera to record whole buildings, details of decorative stone, or any fossils you find.

• •

Chapter Eighteen

What Do I Want to Do with the Rest of My Life?
· ·
Careers in Earth Science

I n Chapter 1, "The Scoop on Earth Science," we talked about the wide variety of subjects and ideas that are under the earth science umbrella. Likewise, careers involving earth science are greatly varied. They range from desk jobs to fieldwork, from hands-on activities to proposing theories, from air analysis to soil science to oceanography. Is there one particular area of earth science that interests you more than another? Maybe it's mapmaking. Or maybe fossil hunting. Take a closer look at some careers in earth science and related fields. Remember that this list is just a sampling of earth science careers and that some of them overlap.

Air Analyst/Air Pollution Control Technician
Air analysts collect air samples. The samples may come from a city, a mine, or a specific area such as a factory neighborhood. Air analysts determine which pollutants are in the air and how much of each pollutant is present. They summarize their findings and issue a report. In their reports they may suggest ways to improve pollution control methods.

Education: Air Analyst: College degree, with strong background in chemistry and mathematics, and mechanical ability.

Air Pollution Control Technician: Accredited two-year program in pollution control technology.

For more information write:
Air Pollution Control Association
P.O. Box 2861
Pittsburgh, PA 15230

Astronomer

Astronomy is one field of science in which amateurs can still make discoveries because there are relatively few professionals in the field. Most professional astronomers do research and/or teach. Some astronomers work at planetariums. They often communicate with other astronomers across the country and around the world.

Education: Graduate degree (master's or doctorate) in astronomy, with a strong background in mathematics, chemistry, physics, and a foreign language.

For more information write:
American Astronomical Society
2000 Florida Avenue, N.W.
Suite 300
Washington, DC 20009

Center for Astrophysics and Space Sciences
60 Garden Street
Cambridge, MA 02138

Cartographer (Mapmaker)

Cartographers use information about the world's surface to create maps that graphically represent what the world looks like. Cartographers use photographs taken from space and survey information collected on the ground to make these visual representations. Today's cartographers also use computers to draw maps and collect and interpret geographic information.

Education: College degree in engineering, physical science, earth science, or geography that includes a strong background in geography, mechanical drawing, and computer science.

For more information write:
American Congress on Surveying and Mapping
210 Little Falls Street
Falls Church, VA 22046

Earth Science Educator

Earth science educators may teach elementary school, middle school, high school, or college or university earth science classes. Educators enjoy working with young people.

Education: College degree and teaching certificate (state-issued) for elementary, middle school, or high school. Graduate degree (master's or doctorate) to teach at a college or university.

For more information write:
National Earth Science Teachers Association
(Address changes every few years. Please check with your science teacher.)

National Science Teachers Association
1742 Connecticut Avenue, N.W.
Washington, DC 20009

Energy Manager

Most energy managers work for large corporations. They study how much their companies spends for energy, what kinds of energy it uses, and what steps it has taken to avoid wasting energy. Energy managers suggest ways that the company can cut its energy costs, such as switching to different energy sources or conserving energy.

Education: College degree in engineering or in the earth or physical sciences.

For more information write:
Association of Energy Engineers
4025 Pleasantdale Road, Suite 420
Atlanta, GA 30340

Environmentalist

Environmentalists record or interpret data on the environment. They may gather data outdoors in a neighborhood; in a city; inside a factory; from water in the lake or river where we swim, boat, or fish; and from the air we breathe. Environmentalists may also help our elected officials write environmental laws.

Most environmentalists work for large consulting firms that support businesses and municipalities in complying with federal and state environmental regulations.

Education: College degree in environmental science or related field with a strong background in chemistry, physics, biology, and management.

For more information write:
National Association of Environmental Professionals
5165 MacArthur Boulevard, N.W.
Washington, DC 20016-3315

Gem Cutter

Gem cutters take rough gemstones that may look like dull pebbles and cut, shape, and polish them until they become beautiful stones that will probably be used in jewelry.

Education: High school diploma. Gem cutters begin as apprentices learning the trade through on-the-job training. They start working with inexpensive stones and as they gain more skill and experience they work their way up to more valuable stones.

For more information write:
Gemological Institute of America
1660 Stewart Street
Santa Monica, CA 90406

Geographer

A geographer's field of study encompasses the environment of the surface of the earth and the relationship of humans to this environment. It includes both physical and cultural geographic features. Physical geographic features involve climate, land and water, and plant and animal life. Cultural geographic features include nations, settlements, lines of communication, transportation, and buildings.

Education: College and graduate degrees. A bachelor's degree with a major in geography is required for most positions as professional geographers. A master's degree or doctorate is necessary for college-level teaching or research jobs.

For more information write:
American Geographical Society
156 Fifth Avenue, Suite 600
New York, NY 10010-7002

Association of American Geographers
1710 16th Street, N.W.
Washington, DC 20009-3198

National Council for Geographic Education
16A Leonard Hall
Indiana University of Pennsylvania
Indiana, PA 15705

National Geographic Society
1600 M Street, N.W.
Washington, DC 20036

Geological Fields

Economic Geologist

Economic geology is the branch of geology that deals with geological materials of economic value to people, such as fuels, metals, nonmetallic minerals, water, and geothermal energy.

Engineering Geologist

Engineering geology, or geological engineering, links mining and civil engineering. It involves the study of soil, rock materials, and groundwater as they affect the planning, design, location, construction, operation, and maintenance of engineering structures.

Environmental Geologist

Environmental geology involves collection and analysis of geological data and its application to problems created by human impact upon the environment. Environmental geology is an interdisciplinary field because it includes areas of related interest in physical, biological, and social sciences.

Geochemist

Geochemists specifically study the distribution and amounts of chemicals in minerals, rocks, soil, life-forms, water, and the atmosphere. Exploration geochemistry (also called geochemical prospecting) involves applying geochemical principles to mineral exploration. Other related fields include sedimentary geochemistry, organic geochemistry, and environmental geochemistry.

Geochronologist

Geochronologists study the history of the earth before man and determine the ages of rocks and landforms. They try to determine the sequence of events that took place on the earth before written records. They also develop theories about the history of continents, oceans, mountain ranges, and mineral deposits.

Geomorphologist

Geomorphology deals with the earth's crust and changes in it. Geomorphologists explain surface landforms in terms of principles of erosion and weathering.

Geophysicist

Geophysics is the study of the earth, its atmosphere and oceans, and its environment in space. (That's a lot, isn't it?) Geophysicists use earth science, mathematics, physics, and chemistry to study things such as the effect of gravity on the earth, seismic waves from earthquakes, and solutions to problems related to searching for oil, gas, water, and ore deposits below the earth's surface.

Mineralogist

Mineralogy deals with minerals in the earth's crust as well as with those found outside the earth, such as lunar samples or meteorites. Mineralogists study the formation, occurrence, chemical and physical properties, composition, and classification of minerals.

Paleontologist

Paleontology is the study of prehistoric life. Paleontologists deal with fossil animals and fossil plants in relation to existing plants and animals. Micropaleontology involves investigation of microscopic fossils.

Paleontologists may be hired by oil and mining companies to identify fossils that are found with or near oil and ore deposits. Museums, colleges, and universities also employ paleontologists.

Petrologist

Petrology deals with the origin, occurrence, structure, and history of rocks, particularly igneous and metamorphic rocks. Petrologists study changes that occur when rocks melt and then recrystallize. They look for changes in the minerals in the rock.

Sedimentologist

Sedimentology is the study of sedimentary deposits on land and in the oceans as well as how they were formed. Sedimentologists also study the sediments that compose sedimentary rocks to learn how they formed and what type of environment the rocks came from.

Seismologist

Seismologists are geologists who study earthquakes and the areas in which they occur. Seismologists study faults and how the earth's crust moves along these faults. Much of a seismologist's work involves interpreting and analyzing data collected by seismographs.

Structural Geologist

Structural geology is concerned with analyzing sedimentary layers of the earth's surface. Structural geologists study changes in rock layers and try to discover what caused the changes. Geologists in the oil and mining industries use structural geology in the search for new deposits and for the safe recovery of oil and ores.

Education: All of these geological fields require bachelor's and/or graduate degrees. A background in geology, physics, mathematics, computer science, and chemistry is desirable. Teaching at a college or university, heading a department, or heading a business requires a doctorate.

For more information write:
American Association of Petroleum Geologists
1444 S. Boulder
Tulsa, OK 74119

American Geological Institute
4220 King Street
Alexandria, VA 22302

American Geophysical Union
2006 Florida Avenue, N.W.
Washington, DC 20009

Association of Engineering Geologists
323 Boston Post Road, Suite 2D
Sudbury, MA 01776

Geological Society of America
3300 Penrose Place
P.O. Box 9140
Boulder, CO 80301

Seismological Society of America
2620 Telegraph Avenue
Berkeley, CA 94704

Society of Exploration Geophysicists
8801 S. Yale Avenue
Tulsa, OK 74137

Hydrologist or Groundwater Professional

Hydrologists deal with the earth's water resource. They examine the characteristics, distribution, and circulation of surface water, groundwater, and atmospheric water.

Groundwater professionals are scientists and other workers who work to locate groundwater and suggest the best ways to use it. Geologists in this field locate the water, civil engineers design the wells and pumps needed to get the water to the surface, and hydrogeologists and geophysicists often test the water to make sure it is safe for the intended use, such as drinking.

Education: Master's or doctorate degree in geology, hydrogeology, or engineering, with a strong background in chemistry, groundwater engineering, and calculus.

For more information write:
Association of Ground Water Scientists and Engineers
6375 Riverside Drive
Dublin, OH 43017

Jeweler

Jewelers make and design rings, necklaces, bracelets, and other pieces of jewelry using precious metals like gold, silver, and platinum. They also work with precious and semiprecious gems such as diamonds, emeralds, and rubies.

Jewelers' activities fall into four categories. Some jewelers perform all these tasks; others specialize in just one or two:

• Cutting and shaping gemstones
• Setting gems into pieces of jewelry
• Designing and producing the settings for the stones
• Repairing jewelry, including resizing rings, and resetting stones

Education: High school diploma. Jewelers learn their craft through on-the-job training or by completing a three- to four-year apprentice-ship program.

For more information write:
Jewelers of America
1271 Avenue of the Americas
New York, NY 10020

Manufacturing Jewelers and Silversmiths of America
The Biltmore Plaza Hotel
Kennedy Plaza
Providence, RI 02903

Landscape Architect

Landscape architects design the outdoor areas around homes, business centers, parks, recreation areas, highways, cemeteries, shopping centers, and so on. Landscape architects deal with the shape of the land, water availability, buildings, shrubbery, plants, and open spaces. They make detailed drawings of what will be done in the areas they design. They get necessary approval from the appropriate government agencies (like city and state governments) to carry out the design.

Education: Bachelor's degree with course work in landscape design, landscape construction, plants, architecture, drawing, natural sciences, civil engineering, English, social sciences, and mathematics.

For more information write:
American Society of Landscape Architects
1733 Connecticut Avenue, N.W.
Washington, DC 20009

Landscaper

Landscapers take care of lawns, gardens, parks, golf courses, shopping-center exteriors, building exteriors, sports playing fields, cemeteries, and so on. The work may include planting trees, shrubs, flowers, and lawns; mowing grass; trimming plants; applying fertilizers, pesticides, and weed killers; removing plant material; watering; and mulching.

Education: High school diploma. The trade may be learned through on-the-job training or attending vocational or technical school. A business license and certification to apply chemicals may be necessary.

For more information write:
Associated Landscape Contractors of America
405 North Washington Street
Falls Church, VA 22046

National Landscape Association
1250 I Street, N.W., Suite 500
Washington, DC 20005

Professional Grounds Management Society
12 Galloway Avenue 1E
Cockeysville, MA 21030

Meteorologist

Meteorologists study the atmosphere and how it behaves, including the physical and chemical processes that occur in the atmosphere. They also study how factors such as pollution influence the atmosphere, weather, and climate. Those who prepare weather forecasts gather atmospheric information from all over the world and then make their forecasts about our daily weather.

Education: College or university degree in meteorology with a strong background in math and science. Meteorological technicians need a high school diploma with appropriate vocational training.

For more information write:
American Meteorological Society
45 Beacon Street
Boston, MA 02108

Mine Inspector

Mine inspectors work in coal mines, ore mines, or quarries. Many large mining companies employ their own inspectors, but many other inspectors work for the federal or state governments.

A mine inspector examines mines to make certain that health and safety regulations are being followed. They test air quality in mines to be sure that they are safe. Mine inspectors may also check the structure of mines for safety. Following their inspections, they prepare reports of their findings.

Education: High school diploma minimum. Experience working in mines is highly desirable, and passing a special career examination is required.

For more information write:
Interagency Board of U.S. Civil Service Examiners for Washington, DC
1900 E Street, N.W.
Washington, DC 20415

Museum Director or Curator

The director or curator of a natural history museum carries many responsibilities, including operational management, planning, obtaining grants, and acquiring exhibits. In deciding what to purchase or acquire through gifts or loans, the curator must evaluate whether new collections will improve the museum's educational and research value. Exhibits may involve many years of planning as well as supervision of the many people involved. The curator must plan toward the ultimate goal of visitor education and enjoyment.

Education: Master's or doctorate degree in museum science that includes internship programs as well as background in management and the subjects covered by the museum you want to work for.

For more information write:
Museum Studies Program
Smithsonian Institution
A + 1 Building, Room 2235
Washington, DC 20560

Oceanographer

Oceanographers study many different aspects of the oceans. Physical oceanographers deal with the physical properties of the oceans, such as water movement, water density, and water temperature. Chemical oceanographers study the chemical makeup of ocean water. Marine biologists study the plants and animals that live in the oceans. Marine geologists study the ocean floor.

Education: Most oceanographers have master's or doctorate degrees.

For more information write:
American Society of Limnology and Oceanography
Virginia Institute of Marine Science
College of William and Mary
Gloucester Point, VA 23062

National Oceanic and Atmospheric Administration
AD 411, 6001 Executive Boulevard
Rockville, MD 20852

Oceanographic Foundation
3979 Rickenbacker Causeway
Virginia Key
Miami, FL 33149

Park Ranger

Park rangers may work in national parks, state parks, or county and local parks. Park rangers help preserve our natural environment, conduct lectures and special hikes, help in planning park activities, enforce park rules and regulations, do bookkeeping, and issue permits to visitors.

Education: Bachelor's degree in natural resource management or recreational resource management.

For more information write:
National Recreation and Park Association
3101 Park Center Drive, 12th Floor
Arlington, VA 22302

U.S. Department of the Interior
National Park Service
P.O. Box 37127
Washington, DC 20013

Range Manager or Conservationist

Range managers may also be called range scientists, range ecologists, or conservationists. A range manager's job is to improve and increase the food supply on ranges. Range managers plan and implement erosion control, work with crop rotation, determine the number and kinds of cattle that can graze on the open range, study plants that grow on the range, control recreation, timber, and fires, and keep track of water reservoirs. Most range managers are employed by the federal government.

Education: Bachelor's degree in range science, soil science, or natural resource management.

For more information write:
Bureau of Land Management
Department of the Interior
Washington, DC 20240

Society for Range Management
1839 York Street
Denver, CO 80206

U.S. Department of Agriculture
Forest Service
P.O. Box 2417
Washington, DC 20013

Soil Conservationist

Soil conservationists assist farmers, ranchers, and engineers in their use of land so that soil doesn't wash away into a river or lake. Soil conservationists may be asked to help stop erosion on a farm or to determine how many cattle can graze without destroying the land. Soil conservationists also help design irrigation systems, dams, and landscaped areas. They can take inventory of an area's soil, water, and vegetation. Most soil conservationists work for the federal or state governments.

Education: Master's degree in agricultural science is best. May also have degree in geology or agronomy.

For more information write:
Soil Conservation Service
U.S. Department of Agriculture
Washington, DC 20013

Soil Scientist

Soil scientists study and classify soils. They prepare maps of an area to show the soil types present. They also work with other scientists in determining the ability of different soils to produce healthy crops. They may work with builders to determine whether the land is firm enough to support proposed buildings and how to prevent erosion.

Education: College or university degree with strong background in agronomy, biology, and mapmaking.

For more information write:
American Society of Agronomy
677 S. Segoe Road
Madison, WI 53711

Surveyor

Surveyors measure the elevation, size, and shape of any part of the earth's surface. Usually they work in surveying teams of three to six people. Based on the information the team obtains, surveyors prepare sketches, maps, and reports describing the land.

Surveyors work outdoors in all kinds of environments. Many surveyors are employed by construction companies or government agencies.

Education: Surveyors need a bachelor's degree in surveying, civil engineering, or engineering. They must be licensed or registered in the state in which they work. A surveyor's helper needs a high school diploma.

For more information write:
American Congress on Surveying and Mapping
210 Little Falls Street
Falls Church, VA 22046

Wastewater Treatment Plant Operator

Wastewater treatment plant operators do just what their title suggests—they operate wastewater treatment plants. They control and maintain equipment that removes pollutants and contaminants from the water. During various steps of the treatment process they take water samples for testing, thus making sure that the cleaning and treatment process is proceeding properly. Wastewater treatment plant operators also regulate the amount of chlorine and other chemicals that are used to purify water.

Education: High school diploma minimum. In most areas, wastewater treatment plant operators must be certified, which usually requires attending classes and/or on-the-job training.

For more information write:
Water Pollution Control Federation
2626 Pennsylvania Avenue, N.W.
Washington, DC 20037

Appendix

●●

Materials and Information

Public Park Facilities

Local, state, provincial, and national parks are excellent sources of information about the natural features of the areas they cover. Park interpretive centers often have displays covering the park's geology. They may be able to supply you with brochures and other printed material on a variety of geological, geographical, and other topics related to earth science.

If your local park system offers a newsletter, subscribe to it. In addition to informative articles, it will probably contain listings of scheduled park activities. They may offer geological hikes, riverbed hikes, or informative presentations by experts in the field.

If you prefer to take a couple of friends and hike on your own, park areas provide trails that may even have signs describing the area's features.

Community Historical Societies

Your town or city may have its own historical society—people interested in preserving local history. Community historical societies are excellent sources of information about the activities of early settlers in the area. They can tell you about any mining, quarrying, or fossil finds that occurred long ago. They can tell you what the first settlers did and how they used the land. Sometimes community historical societies maintain their own museums, which may contain artifacts related to earth science in your neighborhood.

Colleges and Universities

If a nearby college or university has an earth science, geology, or geography department, you should be able to find someone to answer your questions or help you with things like rock and mineral identification. Some colleges and universities also maintain geological or natural history museums.

Museums and Park Facilities

Here is a sampling, by state, of some museums and parks that deal with one or more aspects of earth science, geology, or geography.

ALABAMA

Alabama Mining Museum, Dora
Anniston Museum of Natural History, Anniston
Burritt Museum and Park, Huntsville
Russell Cave National Monument, near Bridgeport
University of Alabama State Museum of Natural History, Tuscaloosa

ALASKA

Alaska State Museum, Juneau
Baranof Museum, Kodiak
Denali National Park
Glacier Bay National Park
Katmai National Park and Preserve
Klondike Gold Rush National Historical Park, Skagway
University of Alaska Museum, Fairbanks

ARIZONA

Arizona Mineral Museum, Phoenix
Arizona-Sonora Desert Museum, Tucson
Carl Hayden Visitor Center, Page
Center for Meteorite Studies, Tempe Chiricahua National Monu-
    ment, Willcox
Grace H. Flandrau Planetarium, Tucson
Grand Canyon National Park

Lowell Observatory, Flagstaff
Museum of Astrogeology—Meteor Crater, Flagstaff
Museum of Northern Arizona, Flagstaff
Organ Pipe Cactus National Monument and Museum, Ajo
Painted Desert, along U.S. Route 66
Petrified Forest National Park, Holbrook
Saguaro National Monument, Tucson
Sunset Crater National Monument, Flagstaff
University of Arizona Mineral Museum, Tucson

ARKANSAS

Arkansas State University Museum, State University
Blanchard Caverns, Mountain View
Crater of Diamonds State Park and Museum, Murfreesboro
Henderson State University Museum, Arkadelphia
Hot Springs National Park
Little Rock Planetarium, University of Arkansas
Southeast Arkansas Arts and Science Center, Pine Bluff
University Museum, University of Arkansas, Fayetteville

CALIFORNIA

Alexander F. Morrison Planetarium, San Francisco
Allison Center for the Study of Paleontology, San Diego
Anza-Borrezo Desert State Park, Borrezo Springs
Cabrillo Marine Museum, San Pedro
California Academy of Science, San Francisco
California Oil Museum, Santa Paula
Children's Museum at La Habra, La Habra
Codding Museum of Natural History, Santa Rosa
Death Valley Museum, Death Valley National Monument, Death
    Valley
Desert Museum, Randsbury
Devils Postpile National Monument, Mammoth Lakes
Diablo Valley College Museum, Pleasant Hill
Fort Roosevelt Natural Science and History Museum, Hanford
Griffith Observatory and Planetarium, Los Angeles
Hi-Desert Nature Museum, Yucca Valley
Josephine D. Randall Junior Museum, San Francisco
Jurupa Mountains Cultural Center, Riverside
Lassen Volcanic National Park, Mineral

Lava Beds National Monument, Tulelake
Lawrence Hall of Science, University of California, Berkeley
Lindsay Museum, Walnut Creek
The Living Desert, Palm Desert
Maturango Museum of the Indian Wells Valley, Ridgecrest
Moorten Botanic Garden and Cactarium, Palm Springs
Morro Bay State Park Museum of Natural History, Morro Bay
Mousley Museum of Natural History, Yucaipa
Museum of Paleontology, University of California, Berkeley
Natural History Foundation of Orange County, Newport Beach
Natural History Museum, San Diego
Natural History Museum of Los Angeles County, Los Angeles
Oakland Museum, Oakland
Pacific Grove Museum of Natural History, Pacific Grove
Palm Springs Desert Museum Inc., Palm Springs Palo Alto Junior
    Museum, Palo Alto
Palomar Observatory, Palomar Mountain
Pinnacles National Monument, Paicines
Plumas County Museum, Quincy
Raymond F. Alf Museum, Claremont
Riverside Municipal Museum, Riverside
Rosicrucian Planetarium and Science Museum, San Jose
Sacramento Science Center and Junior Museum, Sacramento
San Bernardino County Museum, Redland
San Diego Space and Science Foundation, San Diego
San Jacinto Valley Museum, San Jacinto
Santa Barbara Museum of Natural History, Santa Barbara
Santa Monica Mountain National Recreation Area, Woodland Hills
Sequoia and Kings Canyon National Parks, Three Rivers
Tree National Monument, Twentynine Palms
Twentynine Palms Oasis Visitor Center, Joshua
Yosemite Museum, National Park Service, Yosemite National Park
Youth Science Institute, San Jose

COLORADO

Aspen Historical Society Museum, Aspen
Black Canyon of the Gunnison National Monument, Gunnison
Canon City Municipal Museum, Canon City
Colorado National Monument, Fruita
Colorado School of Mines Geology Museum, Golden
Colorado Science Center, Denver

Cripple Creek District Museum Inc., Cripple Creek
Denver Museum of Natural History, Denver
Dinosaur National Monument, Dinosaur
Florissant Fossil Beds National Monument, Florissant
Fort Sedgewick Depot Museum, Julesbury
Great Sand Dunes National Monument, Mosca
Jefferson County Planetarium, Lakewood
Lafayette Miners Museum, Lafayette
Longmont Museum, Longmont
Matchless Mine Museum, Leadville
May Natural History Museum, Colorado Springs
Mesa Verde National Park Museum, Mesa Verde
  National Park
Museum of Western Colorado, Grand Junction
Overland Trail Museum, Sterling
Rifle Creek Museum, Rifle
Rocky Ford Historical Museum, Rocky Ford
Rocky Mountain National Park, Estes Park
Saguache County Museum, Saguache
Salida Museum, Salida
San Miguel County Historical Society Museum, Telluride
State Historical Society of Colorado, Denver
Trinidad State Junior College Museum, Trinidad
University of Colorado Museum, Boulder
White River Museum, Meeker

CONNECTICUT

Bruce Museum, Greenwich
Connecticut State Museum of Natural History, Storr
Dinosaur State Park, Rock Hill
Goshen Historical Society, Goshen
Hidden Valley Nature Center, New Fairfield
Hungerford Outdoor Education Center, Kensington
Nature Center for Environmental Activities Inc., Westport
New Canaan Nature Center, New Canaan
Northeast Audubon Center, Sharon
Old New Gate Prison and Copper Mine, East Granby
Peabody Museum of Natural History, Yale University, New Haven
Science Museum of Connecticut, West Hartford
Stamford Museum and Nature Center, Stamford
Thames Science Center, New London
White Memorial Conservation Center, Inc., Litchfield

DELAWARE

Delaware Museum of Natural History, Wilmington

DISTRICT OF COLUMBIA

Explorers Hall, Washington
National Museum of Natural History, Washington
Rock Creek Nature Center
United States Department of the Interior Museum, Washington

FLORIDA

Biscayne National Park, Homestead
Cedar Key State Museum, Cedar Key
Discovery Center Inc., Fort Lauderdale
Everglades National Park, Homestead
Florida State Museum, Gainesville
Gillespie Museum of Minerals, Stetson University, De Land
Museum of Arts and Science, Daytona Beach
Museum of Science, Miami
Museum of Science and History, Jacksonville
Orlando Science Center Inc., Orlando
Safety Harbor Museum of History and Fine Arts, Inc., Safety Harbor
Science Center of Pinellas County, Saint Petersburg
South Florida Museum and Bishop Planetarium, Bradenton
South Florida Science Museum, West Palm Beach
Tomoka Museum, Ormond Beach
University of South Florida Planetarium, Tampa
Youth Museum of Charlotte County, Punta Gorda

GEORGIA

Augusta Richmond County Museum, Augusta
Brasstown Bald Victor Center, Blairsville
Fermbank Science Center, Atlanta
Georgia Southern Museum, Statesboro
Georgia State Museum of Science and Industry, Atlanta
Lanier Museum of Natural History, Buford
Museum of Arts and Science, Macon
Oatland Island Education Center, Savannah
Panola Mountain State Conservation Park, Stockbridge

Providence Canyon State Park, Fargo
University of Georgia Museum of Natural History, Athens

GUAM

Marianas National Parks Association, Agana

HAWAII

Bishop Museum, Honolulu
Haleakala National Park, Makawao
Hawaii Volcanoes National Park, Kilauea Visitor Center
Kalaupapa National Historical Park, Kalaupapa
Lyman House Memorial Museum, Hilo
Waikiki Aquarium, Honolulu

IDAHO

Craters of the Moon National Monument, Arco
Idaho Museum of Natural History, Pocatello
Intermountain Cultural Center and Museum, Weiser
Oakley Pioneer Museum, Oakley
Owyhee County Historical Museum, Murphy
Saint Gertrude's Museum, Cottonwood

ILLINOIS

Adler Planetarium, Chicago
Burpee Museum of Natural History, Rockford
Cernan Earth and Space Center, River Grove
Elgin Public Museum, Elgin
Evanston Environmental Association, Evanston
Field Museum of Natural History, Chicago
Fryxell Geology Museum, Rock Island
Illinois State Museum, Springfield
Illinois State University Museum, Normal
Iroquois County Historical Society Museum, Watseka
John Deere Planetarium, Rock Island
John G. Shedd Aquarium, Chicago
Jurica Natural History Museum, Lisle
Kane County Forest Preserve and Fabyan Villa, Geneva
Lakeview Museum of Arts and Science, Peoria

Lizzadro Museum of Lapidary Arts, Elmhurst
Museum of the Chicago Academy of Sciences, Chicago
Museum of Natural History, University of Illinois, Urbana
Museum of Science and Industry, Chicago
Nauvoo Historical Society Museum, Nauvoo
Quincy Museum of Natural History and Art, Quincy
Starved Rock State Park, Utica
University Museum, Southern Illinois University, Carbondale
Village of Elsah Museum, Elsah

INDIANA

Evansville Museum of Arts and Science, Evansville
Historic New Harmony, Inc., New Harmony
Indiana Dunes National Lakeshore, Porter
Indiana State Museum, Indianapolis
J. J. Holcomb Observatory and Planetarium, Indianapolis
Joseph Moore Museum, Richmond
Upper Wabash Basin Regional Resource Center, Huntington

IOWA

Grout Museum of History and Science, Waterloo
Hartman Reserve Nature Center, Cedar Falls
Iowa State Historical Museum, Des Moines
Iowa State Museum, Des Moines
Putnam Museum, Davenport
Sanford Museum and Planetarium, Cherokee
Science Center of Iowa, Des Moines
Sioux City Public Museum, Sioux City
University of Iowa Museum of Natural History, Iowa City
University of Northern Iowa Museum, Cedar Falls

KANSAS

Benedictine College Museum, Atchison Fick Fossil and
    History Museum, Oakley
Fort Hays State Museum, Hays
Kansas Cosmosphere and Space Center, Hutchinson
Kauffman Museum, North Newton
Lake Afton Public Observatory, Wichita
McPherson County Old Mill Museum and Park, Lindsborg

McPherson Museum, McPherson
Museum of Natural History, Lawrence
Post Rock Museum, La Crosse
Sternberg Memorial Museum, Hays

KENTUCKY

Berea College Museum, Berea
Hardin Planetarium, Bowling Green
Joseph Rauch Memorial Planetarium, Louisville
Living Arts and Science Center, Inc., Lexington
Mammoth Cave National Park, Mammoth Cave
Museum of History and Science, Louisville

LOUISIANA

Grindstone Bluff Museum and Environmental Education Center,
  Shreveport
Lafayette Natural History Museum and Planetarium, Lafayette
Louisiana Nature and Science Center, Inc., New Orleans
L.S.U. Museum of Geoscience, Baton Rouge

MAINE

Acadia National Park, Bar Harbor
Castine Scientific Society, Castine
Maine State Museum, Augusta
Nylander Museum, Caribou
Wilson Museum, Castine

MARYLAND

Howard B. Owens Science Center, Lanham-Seabrook
Maryland Academy of Sciences, Baltimore
National Aquarium, Baltimore

MASSACHUSETTS

Arcadia Nature Center and Wildlife Sanctuary, Easthampton
Cape Cod Museum of Natural History, Brewster
Cape Cod National Seashore, South Wellfleet

Historical, Natural History, and Library Society of Natick, South Natick
Mineralogical Museum of Harvard University, Cambridge
New England Aquarium Corporation, Boston
Pratt Museum of Natural History, Amherst
Springfield Science Museum, Springfield

MICHIGAN

Abrams Planetarium, Michigan State University, East Lansing
A. E. Seamen Mineralogical Museum, Houghton
Argus Planetarium, Ann Arbor
Belle Isle Nature Center, Detroit
Center for Cultural and Natural History, Mount Pleasant
Cranbrook Institute of Science, Bloomfield Hills
Detroit Science Center, Detroit
Dinosaur Gardens, Inc., Ossineke
Drummond Island Historical Museum, Drummond Island
Great Lakes Area Paleontological Museum, Traverse City
The Hands-On Museum, Ann Arbor
Iron Mountain Iron Mines, Vulcan
Isle Royale National Park, Houghton
Kalamazoo Nature Center Inc., Kalamazoo
Kensington Metro Park Nature Center, Milford
Kingman Museum of Natural History, Battle Creek
Robert T. Langway Planetarium, Flint
Sarett Nature Center, Benton Harbor
Sloan Museum, Flint
University of Michigan Natural Science Museum, Ann Arbor

MINNESOTA

Cook County Museum, Grand Marais
Grant County Historical Society, Elbow Lake
James Ford Bell Museum of Natural History, Minneapolis
Lyon County Historical Society, Marshall
Science Museum of Minnesota, Saint Paul
Voyageurs National Park, South International Falls
Walker Museum, Walker
Yellow Medicine County Historical Museum, Granite Falls

MISSISSIPPI

Dunn-Seiler Museum, Mississippi State University
John Martin Frazier Museum of Natural History, Hattiesburg
Mississippi Museum of Natural Science, Jackson
William M. Colmer Visitor Center, Ocean Springs

MISSOURI

Babler Nature Interpretive Center, Chesterfield
Ed Clark Museum of Missouri Geology, Rolla
Kansas City Museum, Kansas City
Maramea Museum, The James Foundation, Saint James
Nature Interpretive Center, Lebanon
Rockwoods Reservation, Glencoe
Saint Louis Science Center, Saint Louis
Stephens Museum of Natural History and United Methodist Museum
    of Missouri, Fayette
Tri-State Mineral Museum, Joplin
University of Missouri-Rolla Minerals Museum, Rolla

MONTANA

Carter County Museum, Ekalaka
Central Montana Museum, Lewistown
Earth Science Museum, Loma
Fort Peck Museum, Fort Peck
Glacier National Park
McCone County Museum, Circle
Mineral Museum, Butte
Museum of the Rockies, Bozeman
Northern Montana College Collection, Havre

NEBRASKA

Agate Fossil Beds National Monument, Harrison
Cass County Historical Society Museum, Plattsmouth
CSC Earth Science Museum, Chadron
Fort Kearney Museum, Kearney
Fort Niobrara National Wildlife Refuge, Valentine

Historical Society of Garden County, Oshkosh
University of Nebraska State Museum, Lincoln

NEVADA

Churchill County Museum and Archive, Fallon
Fleischmann Planetarium, Reno
Great Basin National Park, Baker
Lake Mead National Recreation Area, Boulder City
Lost City Museum, Overton
Mackay School of Mines Museum, Reno
Museum of Natural History, University of Nevada, Las Vegas
Nevada State Museum, Carson City
Nevada State Museum and Historical Society, Las Vegas
White Pine Public Museum, Ely

NEW HAMPSHIRE

Annie E. Woodman Institute, Dover
Montshire Museum of Science, Hanover
Mount Washington Museum, Gorham

NEW JERSEY

Cora Hartshorn Arboretum, Short Hills
Environmental Education Center, Somerset County Park Commission, Basking Ridge
Meadowlands Museum, Rutherford
Morris Museum, Morristown
Newark Museum, Newark
New Jersey State Museum, Trenton
Paterson Museum, Paterson
Poricy Park Nature Center, Middletown
Princeton University Museum of Natural History, Princeton
Trailside Nature and Science Center, Mountainside

NEW MEXICO

Bandelier National Monument, Los Alamos
Blackwater Draw Museum, Portales
Capulin Mountain National Monument, Capulin
Carlsbad Caverns National Park, Carlsbad

Carlsbad Museum and Art Center, Carlsbad
El Morro National Monument, Ramah
Ghost Ranch Living Museum, Abiquin
Governor Bent Museum, Taos
Guadalupe Mountains National Park, Carlsbad
Institute of Meteoritics Meteorite Museum, Albuquerque
New Mexico Bureau of Mines Mineral Museum, Socorro
Red Rock Museum, Church Rock
The Space Center, Alamogordo
Tucumcari Historical Research Institute
White Sands National Monument, Alamogordo

NEW YORK

American Museum—Hayden Planetarium, New York
American Museum of Natural History, New York
Bear Mountain Trailside Museum and Zoo, Bear Mountain
Buffalo Museum of Science, Buffalo
Children's Museum of History, Natural History and Science at Utica,
    New York
Gregory Museum Long Island Earth Science Center, Hicksville
Museum of the Hudson Highlands, Cornwall-on-Hudson
Museum of Long Island Natural Science, Stony Brook
Museum of Natural History, Pawling
Newark Valley Historical Society, Newark Valley
New York State Museum, Albany
Paleontological Research Institution, Ithaca
Petrified Creatures Museum of Natural History, Richfield Springs
Planetarium of the Vanderbilt Museum, Centerport
Rochester Museum and Science Center, Rochester
Rochester Museum Strasenburgh Planetarium, Rochester
Schoellkopf Geological Museum, Niagara Falls
Science Museum, Cortland
Trailside Nature Museum, Cross River

NORTH CAROLINA

Art and Science Center, Statesville
Catawba Science Center, Hickory
Cliffs of the Neuse State Park, Seven Springs
Davidson County Historical Museum, Lexington
Discover Place, Charlotte

High Point Environmental Education Center, High Point
Horizons Unlimited Supplementary Education Center, Salisbury
Lake Waccamaw Depot Museum, Lake Waccamaw
Memorial Mineral Museum, Asheville
Museum of North Carolina Minerals, Spruce Pine
Natural Science Center of Greensboro, Inc., Greensboro
Nature Museum, Charlotte
Nature Science Center, Winston-Salem
North Carolina State Museum, Raleigh
Reed Gold Mine State Historic Site, Stanfield
Schiele Museum of Natural History and Planetarium, Inc., Gastonia

NORTH DAKOTA

State Historical Society of North Dakota, Bismarck
Theodore Roosevelt National Park—Visitor Center, Medora

OHIO

Allen County Museum, Lima
Center of Science and Industry of the Franklin County Historical
    Society, Columbus
Cincinnati Museum of Natural History and Planetarium, Cincinnati
Cleveland Museum of Natural History, Cleveland
Ehrhart Museum, Antwerp
Firelands Historical Society Museum, Norwalk
Flint Ridge State Memorial Museum, Glenford
Fort Hill Museum, Hillsboro
Jones Collection of Minerals and Biology Museum, Tiffin
Lake Erie Nature and Science Center, Bay Village
NASA Lewis Research Center Visitor Information Center, Cleveland
Ohio Historical Center, Columbus
Orton Geological Museum, Ohio State University, Columbus
Toledo Museum of Natural Science, Toledo
Trailside Nature Center and Museum, Cincinnati
University of Cincinnati Geology Museum, Cincinnati
Weitkamp Observatory and Planetarium, Westerville

OKLAHOMA

A. D. Buck Museum of Natural History and Science, Tonkawa
Connors State College Museum, Warner

Kerr Museum, Poteau
Museum of the Western Prairie, Altus
No Man's Land Historical Museum, Goodwell
Northwestern Oklahoma State University Museum, Alva
Stephens County Historical Museum, Duncan
Stovall Museum of Science and History, Stovall
Tucker Tower Nature Center, Ardmore

OREGON

A. R. Bowman Memorial Museum, Prineville
Children's Museum, Portland
Crater Lake National Park, Crater Lake
Grant County Historical Museum, Canyon City
Harney County Historical Museum, Burns
Josephine County Kerbyville Museum, Kerby
Oregon Museum of Science and Industry, Portland
Tillamook County Pioneer Museum, Tillamook

PENNSYLVANIA

Academy of Natural Science of Philadelphia, Philadelphia
All-College Museums, West Chester University, West Chester
Carnegie Museum of Natural History, Carnegie Institute, Pittsburgh
Cornwall Iron Furnace, Cornwall
Erie Historical Museum and Planetarium, Erie
Franklin Institute Science Museum and Planetarium, Philadelphia
Gilman Museum, Hellertown
Museum of Anthracite Mining, Ashland
North Museum of Franklin and Marshall College, Lancaster
Presque Isle State Park, Erie
Reading School District Planetarium, Reading
Riverbend Environmental Education Center, Gladwyne
Schuylkill Valley Nature Center, Philadelphia
Spring Museum, Spring
Wyoming Historical and Geological Society, Wilkes-Barre

RHODE ISLAND

Roger Williams Park Museum, Providence

SOUTH CAROLINA

Charleston Museum, Charleston
Congaree Swamp National Monument, Columbia
Howell Memorial Planetarium, Hamston
The Museum, Greenwood
Myrtle Beach State Park Nature Center, Myrtle Beach
South Carolina State Museum, Columbia
University of South Carolina McKissick Museum, Columbia

SOUTH DAKOTA

Badlands National Park, Interior
Badlands Petrified Gardens, Kadoka
Bear Butte State Park Visitors Center, Sturgis
Black Hills Petrified Forest, Piedmont
Custer County 1881 Courthouse Museum, Custer
Douglas County Museum and Country School, Armour
Museum of Geology, South Dakota School of Mines and Technology,
    Rapid City
Pioneer Auto Museum, Murdo
Wind Cave National Park, Hot Springs

TENNESSEE

Chattanooga Nature Center, Chattanooga
Cumberland and Science Museum, Nashville
Estelle Carmack Bandy Children's Museum, Kingsport
Herbarium Museum of Rhodes College, Memphis
Students' Museum, Inc., Knoxville

TEXAS

Archer County Museum, Archer
Austin Nature Center, City of Austin Parks and Recreation
    Department, Austin
Big Bend National Park, Big Bend
Brazosport Museum of Natural Science, Brazosport
Brazos Valley Museum, Bryan
Carson County Square House Museum, Panhandle
Colorado City Historical Museum, Colorado City
Corpus Christi Museum, Corpus Christi

Crockett County Museum, Ozona
Dallas Museum of Natural History/Dallas Aquarium, Dallas
El Paso Centennial Museum, University of Texas, El Paso
Environmental Science Center, Houston
Fiedler Memorial Museum, Seguin
Fort Worth Museum of Science and History, Fort Worth
Heard Natural Science Museum and Wildlife Sanctuary, Inc.,
    McKinney
Houston Museum of Natural Science, Houston
John E. Conner Museum, Kingville
Llando Estacado Museum, Plainview
Midland County Historical Museum, Midland
The Museum of Texas Tech University, Lubbock
NASA Lyndon B. Johnson Space Center, Houston
Padre Island National Seashore, Corpus Christi
Panhandle-Plains Historical Museum, Canyon
Rankin Museum, Rankin
Roberts County Museum, Miami
Somervell County Museum, Glen Pose
Southwest Museum of Science and Technology, The Science Place,
    Dallas
Strecker Museum, Waco
Texas Memorial Museum, Austin
Texas Zoo, Victoria
Western Company Museum, Fort Worth
Youth Cultural Center, Waco

UTAH

Arches National Park, Moab
Bryce Canyon National Park Visitor Center, Bryce Canyon
Capitol Reef National Park Visitor Center, Torrey
Cedar Breaks National Monument, Cedar City
Dan O'Laurie Museum, Moab
Dead Horse Point State Park, Moab
Fairview Museum of History and Art, Fairview
Natural Bridges National Monument, Blanding
Prehistoric Museum of the College of Eastern Utah, Price
Timpanogos Cave National Monument, American Fork
Utah Field House of Natural History State Park, Vernal
Utah Museum of Natural History, Salt Lake City
Zion National Park Museum, Springdale

VERMONT

Green Mountain National Forest

VIRGINIA

Arlington Historical Museum, Arlington
Chesapeake Planetarium, Chesapeake
D. Ralph Hostetter Museum of Natural History, Harrisonburg
John C. Wells Planetarium, Harrisonburg
M. T. Brackbill Planetarium, Harrisonburg
NASA Langley Visitor Center, Hampton
Oyster Museum of Chinco, Chincoteague
Pittsylvania County School Planetarium, Chatham
Ramsay Nature Center, Alexandria
Sale Planetarium, Lexington
Science Museum of Virginia, Richmond
Shenandoah National Park, Luray
Virginia Museum of Natural History, Martinsville

WASHINGTON

Adam East Museum, Moses Lake
Mount Rainier National Park, Ashford
North Cascades National Park Service Complex
Pacific Science Center, Seattle
Pioneer Memorial Museum, Port Angeles

WEST VIRGINIA

Geology Museum, Huntington
Sunrise Museum, Charleston

WISCONSIN

Greene Memorial Museum, University of Wisconsin, Milwaukee
Henry S. Reuss Ice Age Visitor Center, Campbellsport
Kenosha Public Museum, Kenosha
Milwaukee Public Museum, Milwaukee
Museum of Natural History, Stevens Point

Neville Public Museum of Brown County, Green Bay
New London Public Museum, New London
Peninsula State Park, Fish Creek
Platteville Mining Museum, Platteville
Saint Croix National Riverway, Saint Croix Falls
Sauk County Historical Museum, Baraboo
Thunderbird Museum, Merrillan
University of Wisconsin Arboretum, Madison

WYOMING

Devils Tower Visitor Center, Devils Tower
Fremont County Pioneer Museum, Lander
Geological Museum, The University of Wyoming, Laramie
Grand Teton National Park, Moose
Greybull Museum, Greybull
Wyoming State Museum, Cheyenne
Yellowstone National Park, Yellowstone Park

Finding Maps

U.S. GEOLOGICAL SURVEY (USGS)

U.S. Geological Survey
Map Distribution Center
Federal Center, Building 41
Box 25286
Denver, CO 80225
(303) 236–7477

The USGS creates and produces about sixty thousand topographic maps covering the entire country in a variety of scales. State-by-state indexes of topographic, geological, and general maps, national park indexes, listings of maps by category, indexes by map scale, price lists, and order forms are available free upon request from the address above or from the following regional public information offices:

USGS Public Inquiries Office
4230 University Drive
Room 101
Anchorage, AK 99501

USGS Public Inquiries Office
Building 3, Room 122, Mail Stop 533
345 Middlefield Road
Menlo Park, CA 94025

USGS Public Inquiries Office
169 Federal Building
1961 Stout Street
Denver, CO 80294

USGS Public Inquiries Office
1-C-45 Federal Building
1100 Commerce Street
Dallas, TX 75242

USGS Public Inquiries Office
8105 Federal Building
125 South State Street
Salt Lake City, UT 84138

USGS Public Inquiries Office
503 National Center, Room 1-C-402
12201 Sunrise Valley Drive
Reston, VA 22092

Residents of Alaska may purchase maps of their state from the

Alaska Distribution Section
U.S. Geological Survey
New Federal Building
Box 12
101 Twelfth Avenue
Fairbanks, AK 99701
(907) 456-7535

NATIONAL CARTOGRAPHIC INFORMATION CENTER (NCIC)

National Cartographic Information Center
507 National Center
12201 Sunrise Valley Drive
Reston, VA 22092
(703) 860-6045

Information, indexes, and USGS pamphlets are available from the NCIC, which is a part of the USGS. The NCIC is probably the best source of information on maps produced or distributed by the federal government. The NCIC gathers, organizes, and distributes maps, charts, aerial photographs, digital map data, geodetic control data, geographic data, and satellite products.

EROS DATA CENTER

User Services Section
EROS Data Center
U.S. Geological Survey
Sioux Falls, SD 57198
(605) 594-6151

Another USGS branch, EROS Data Center, distributes aerial photographs, photo maps, and Landsat images.

GEOLOGICAL SURVEY OF CANADA

Geological Survey of Canada
601 Booth Street
Ottawa, Ontario
Canada K1A 0E8
(613) 995-4342

The Geological Survey of Canada publishes geological maps. They offer free pamphlets and posters (one copy per person, please) on rocks, minerals, gemstones, meteorites, fossils, and fossils of the Burgess shales.

CANADA MAP OFFICE

Canada Map Office
130 Bentley Road
Nepean, Ontario
Canada K1A 0E9
(613) 952-7000

Canadian topographic maps are available from the Canada Map Office.

STATE GEOLOGICAL SURVEYS

Contact your state geological survey for its list of materials and maps.

Geological Survey of Alabama
420 Hackberry Lane
P.O. Box 0
Tuscaloosa, AL 35486-9780
(205) 349-2852

Division of Geological and Geophysical Surveys
3700 Airport Way
Fairbanks, AK 99709
(907) 451-2760

Arizona Geological Survey
845 North Park Avenue
Tucson, AZ 85719
(602) 882-4795

Arkansas Geological Commission
3815 West Roosevelt Road
Little Rock, AR 72204
(501) 324-9165

California Division of Mines and Geology
1416 Ninth Street, Room 1320
Sacramento, CA 95814
(916) 445-1923

Colorado Geological Survey
1313 Sherman Street, Room 718
Denver, CO 80203
(303) 866-2611

Connecticut Geological and Natural History Survey
165 Capitol Avenue, Room 553
Hartford, CT 06106
(203) 566-3540

Delaware Geological Survey
University of Delaware
Newark, DE 19716
(302) 451-2833

Florida Geological Survey
903 West Tennessee Street
Tallahassee, FL 32304-7795
(904) 488-9380

Georgia Geologic Survey
19 Martin Luther King, Jr., S.W.
Atlanta, GA 30334
(404) 656-3214

Department of Land and Natural Resources
Division of Water Resource Management
P.O. Box 373
Honolulu, HI 96809
(808) 548-7533

Idaho Geological Survey
University of Idaho
Morrill Hall, Room 332
Moscow, ID 83843-4199
(208) 885-7991

Illinois State Geological Survey
Natural Resources Building
615 East Peabody Drive, Room 121
Champaign, IL 61820
(217) 353-4747

Indiana Geological Survey
611 North Walnut Grove
Bloomington, IN 47405
(812) 335-2862

Geological Survey Bureau
123 North Capitol Street
Iowa City, IA 52242
(319) 335-1575

Kansas Geological Survey
1930 Constant Avenue, Campus West
Lawrence, KS 66047
(913) 864-3965

Kentucky Geological Survey
228 Mining and Mineral Resources Building
University of Kentucky
Lexington, KY 40506-0107
(606) 257-5863

Louisiana Geological Survey
Department of Natural Resources
Box G, University Station
Baton Rouge, LA 70893
(504) 388-5320

Maine Geological Survey
Department of Conservation
State House Station 22
Augusta, ME 04333
(207) 289-2801

Maryland Geological Survey
2300 Saint Paul Street
Baltimore, MD 21218
(301) 554-5500

Executive Office of Environmental Affairs
100 Cambridge Street, Room 2000
Boston, MA 02202
(617) 727-9800

Michigan Department of Natural Resources
Box 30028
Lansing, MI 48909
(517) 344-6923

Minnesota Geological Survey
2642 University Avenue
Saint Paul, MN 55114-1057
(612) 627-4780

Mississippi Office of Geology
P.O. Box 20307
Jackson, MS 39289
(601) 961-5500

Division of Geology and Land Survey
111 Fairgrounds Road
P.O. Box 250
Rolla, MO 65401
(314) 364-1752

Montana Bureau of Mines and Geology
Montana College of Mineral Science and Technology
Butte, MT 59701
(406) 496-4181

Conservation and Survey Division
The University of Nebraska
901 North 17th Street
113 Nebraska Hall
Lincoln, NE 68588-0517
(402) 472-3471

Nevada Bureau of Mines and Geology
University of Nevada-Reno
Reno, NV 89557-0088
(702) 784-6691

Department of Environmental Services
6 Hazen Street
P.O. Box 95
Concord, NH 03301
(603) 271-3503

New Jersey Geological Survey
Division of Science and Research
CN-029
Trenton, NJ 08625
(609) 292-1185

New Mexico Bureau of Mines and Mineral Resources
Campus Station
Socorro, NM 87801
(505) 835-5420

New York State Geological Survey
3136 Cultural Education Center
Albany, NY 12230
(518) 474-5816

North Carolina Geological Survey Section
P.O. Box 27687
Raleigh, NC 27611-7687
(919) 733-2423

North Dakota Geological Survey
University Station
Grand Fork, ND 58202-8156
(701) 777-2231

Ohio Division of Geological Survey
4383 Fountain Square Drive
Columbus, OH 43224-1362
(614) 265-6605

Oklahoma Geological Survey
Energy Center, Room N-131
100 East Boyd
Norman, OK 73019-0628
(405) 325-3031

Department of Geology and Mineral Industries, Suite 965
80 NE Oregon Street, #28
Portland, OR 97232
(503) 731-4100

Pennsylvania Geological Survey
P.O. Box 2357
Harrisburg, PA 17120
(717) 787-2169

Servicio Geologica de Puerto Rico
Apartado 5886
Puerta de Tierra
San Juan, PR 00906
(809) 722-2526

University of Rhode Island
Department of Geology
Kingston, RI 02881
(401) 792-2184

Appendix ● 209

South Carolina Geological Survey
5 Geology Road
Columbia, SC 29210-9998
(803) 737-9440

South Dakota Geological Survey
Joe Foss Building
523 East Capitol Avenue
Pierre, SD 57501
(605) 677-5227

Division of Geology
701 Broadway, Room B30
Nashville, TN 37243-0445
(615) 742-6689

Bureau of Economic Geology
Balcones Research Center
University Station, Box X
Austin, TX 78713-7508
(512) 471-1534

Utah Geological Survey
2363 Foothill Drive
Salt Lake City, UT 84109-1491
(801) 467-7970

Agency of Natural Resources Center Building
103 South Main Street
Waterbury, VT 05676
(802) 244-5164

Virginia Division of Mineral Resources
P.O. Box 3667
Charlottesville, VA 22903
(804) 293-5121

Caribbean Research Institute
College of the Virgin Islands
St. Thomas, VI 00801
(809) 774-9200

Division of Geology and Earth Resources
Mail Stop PY 12
Olympia, WA 98504
(206) 753-5327

West Virginia Geological and Economic Survey
P.O. Box 879
Morgantown, WV 26507-0879

Wisconsin Geological and Natural History Survey
University of Wisconsin
3817 Mineral Point Road
Madison, WI 53705
(608) 263-7384

Geological Survey of Wyoming
P.O. Box 3008
University Station
Laramie, WY 82071
(307) 766-2286

Science Supplies

Carolina Biological Supply Company
2700 York Road
Burlington, NC 27215

Dino Productions
Earth Science Supplies
P.O. Box 3004
Englewood, CO 80155-3004

Edmund Scientific
101 E. Gloucester Pike
Barrington, NJ 08007-1380

NASCO
901 Junesville Avenue
P.O. Box 901
Fort Atkinson, WI 53538-0901

Ward's Natural Science Establishment, Inc.
5100 West Henrietta Road
P.O. Box 92912
Rochester, NY 14692-9012

Meteorite Dealers

Bethany Trading Company
P.O. Box 3726
New Haven, CT 06525

David New
P.O. Box 278
Anacortes, WA 98221

Oklahoma Meteorite Laboratory
P.O. Box 1923
Stillwater, OK 74076

Acknowledgments
●●

We wish to thank the following people and organizations that provided assistance, materials, and/or photographs:

Public Affairs Office, Department of the Army, Waterways Experiment Station, Corps of Engineers, Vicksburg, MS.

Dr. Martin Prinz, Department of Mineral Sciences, American Museum of Natural History, New York, NY.

Geological Survey of Canada, Ottawa, Ontario.

U.S. Department of the Interior, Geological Survey, Denver, CO.

New York State Department of Economic Development, Albany, NY.

U.S. Department of the Interior, National Park Service, Washington, DC.

Center for Meteorite Studies, Arizona State University, Tempe, AZ.

Field Museum of Natural History, Chicago, IL.

National Museum of Natural History, Smithsonian Institution, Washington, DC.

The Natural History Museum, London, England.

Oklahoma Meteorite Laboratory, Stillwater, OK.

Western Australian Museum, Perth, Western Australia.

The Canadian Consulate, Cleveland, OH.

Index

●●

North America, 97, 150, 166
Nurek Dam, 57

obsidian, 121
oceanographers, 179
O horizon, 69
oil, 130
Oklahoma Meteorite Laboratory Inc.,
    Stillwater, OK, 154
Oroville Dam, 57
orthoclase (potassium), 163
orthoquartzite, 164
oxbow lake, 49

Paddle to the Sea (Holling), 34
"Painted Desert" sandstone, 164
paleontologists, 174
Palestine, 166
pallasites, 149
Paraná River, 36, 57, 58
parent material, 65, 84, 91
park rangers, 180
Pati Dam, 57
pearly minerals, 103
Peary, Robert E., 143
pedalfers, 91–92
pedocals, 92
permeability and retentivity, 77–79 per-
    mineralized fossils, 129
Peters, Arno, 8
petrologists, 174
pH. *See* acid-alkaline balance (pH)
phosphorus (P), 87
Platte River, 49
plutonic (intrusive) rocks, 116, 131
pollution, 34
pore space: in dimension stone, 162; in
    soil, 72, 76–77
portland cement, 165–66
potassium (P), 87
pumice, 116, 121, 122
pyrite, 105
pyrrhotite, 104, 108

quadrangle, 12, 25
quartz, 100, 102, 163
quartzite, 118
quartz sandstone, 164

Quebec, 41, 58
Quill, Lake, 36

raised relief maps, 25
Rancho La Brea, California (La Brea
    Tar Pits), 130
Rand McNally, 7
range managers or conservationists,
    180
regional soils, 91–92
regolith, 65, 131
relief maps, 25–29; raised, 25; visual, 25
replacement fossils, 129
*Reports on the Fossils in the Vicinity of
    Paris* (Lamarck), 128
resinous minerals, 102
retentivity and permeability, 77–79
reverse faults, 158
rhombohedral cleavage, 105
Rio Caroní, Venezuela, 36
rivers, 36–37; braided channels, 49;
    dams, 55–58; deltas, 50, 53–54; dis-
    solved materials transported by, 41–
    42, 45–46; endangerment of, 59; and
    erosion, 41–42; levees and
    floodplains, 50, 52–53; meanders,
    48–49; and stream tables, 37–40, 47–
    48, 51–55
Robinson, Arthur, 8
rock-carving maps, 5, 6
rocks, 115–25; acid test for, 123; cata-
    loging, 120; classification, 116–18;
    geodes, 118–19; grain in, 120–22;
    identification, 119–24; igneous, 116,
    121, 122, 124; metamorphic, 118,
    125; sedimentary, 117, 125
Rogunskaya Dam, 57

Saint Ann's Church, Cleveland Heights,
    OH, 167
Saint Lawrence River, 41
Salem (Indiana) Limestone, 118, 167
San Andreas Fault, 157
sand, 71, 73, 75, 76, 165
sandstone, 117, 118, 121, 131, 161,
    162, 165; varieties, 164. *See also* ur-
    ban geology
satellite imagery, 6